MW01223337

LITURGY FOR THE PEOPLE OF GOD: A TRILOGY

Volume One: Foundations of Vatican II Liturgy
Volume Two: The Celebration of the Eucharist
Volume Three: Sacraments and Other Matters Liturgical

LITURGY FOR THE PEOPLE OF GOD: A TRILOGY

Volume One: Foundations of Vatican II Liturgy
Volume Two: The Celebration of the Eucharist
Volume Three: Sacraments and Other Matters Liturgical

"God does not need liturgy; people do."

"By your gift I will utter your praise in the vast assembly."
(Psalm 22:26)

CHARLES E. MILLER, C.M.

ALBA·HOUSE   NEW·YORK

SOCIETY OF ST. PAUL, 2187 VICTORY BLVD., STATEN ISLAND, NEW YORK 10314

ST PAULS

Library of Congress Cataloging-in-Publication Data

Miller, Charles Edward, 1929-
   Liturgy for the people of God : A trilogy / Charles E. Miller.
      p. cm.
   Includes bilbiograhical references.
   Contents: vol. 1. Foundations of Vatican II liturgy — vol. 2. The celebration of the
   Eucharist — vol. 3. Sacraments and other matters liturgical.
      ISBN: 0-8189-0881-5 (alk. paper)
         1. Catholic Church—Liturgy. 2. Catholic Church—Doctrines.   I. Title.

BX1970.M525 2000
264'.02—dc21   00-037208

   ISBN: 0-8189-0878-5 Foundations of Vatican II Liturgy, Volume 1
   ISBN: 0-8189-0879-3 The Celebration of the Eucharist, Volume 2
   ISBN: 0-8189-0880-7 Sacraments and Other Matters Liturgical, Volume 3
   ISBN: 0-8189-0881-5 Liturgy for the People of God, A Trilogy, 3 Volume Set

Imprimi Potest:
Bernard J. Quinn, CM
Provincial, Province of the West

Nihil Obstat:
Rev. Richard Albarano
Censor Deputatus

Imprimatur:
His Eminence Cardinal Roger Mahoney
Archbishop of Los Angeles
March 10, 2000

The *Nihil Obstat* and *Imprimatur* are official declarations that the work contains nothing
contrary to Faith and Morals. It is not implied thereby that those granting the *Nihil Obstat*
and *Imprimatur* agree with the contents, statements, or opinions expressed.

Produced and designed in the United States of America by the
Fathers and Brothers of the Society of St. Paul,
2187 Victory Boulevard, Staten Island, New York 10314-6603,
as part of their communications apostolate.

ISBN: 0-8189-0880-7

Printing Information:

Current Printing - first digit   1   2   3   4   5   6   7   8   9   10

Year of Current Printing - first year shown

2001   2002   2003   2004   2005   2006   2007   2008   2009   2010

VOLUME THREE:
SACRAMENTS AND OTHER MATTERS LITURGICAL

"Out of the cloud came a voice which said, 'This is my beloved Son on whom my favor rests. Listen to him.'"
(Matthew 17:5)

Table of Contents

Foreword

I HAVE NEVER READ A BOOK on liturgy which made me laugh. I hope that the one you are about to read will give you a few chuckles. I have studied a number of books on liturgy which seemed so abstruse that I did not fathom what they intended to teach. I hope that what I present is clear and straightforward. I have come across a lot of articles on liturgy, especially recently, which were so esoteric that I could find no application for what they presented. I have tried to make this trilogy spiritually practical.

Liturgy embraces not only the Eucharist but also the six other sacraments, the Liturgical Year, and the Liturgy of the Hours. Liturgy is from the Greek which means "the work of the people." That tells us that liturgy requires effort from everyone in church. The documents call that effort "full, active participation." This participation is not only external but internal. Liturgy involves our hearts as well as our voices, our souls as well as our bodies, our feelings as well as our minds. Liturgy is the highest form of prayer possible to us since it is the worship which Christ offers to his Father in union with all the people who are united by the power of the Holy Spirit as one body in his Church.

The contents of this trilogy have been part of my life for a long time. I hope they will become part of your life too. I thought them of such importance that I considered it worthwhile to put forth even my feeble efforts to present them to anyone who is open to the truth that active participation in the liturgy is the indispensable source of the true Christian spirit.

I intend this work to be a pastoral presentation on pastoral liturgy. It does not consider monastic or experimental liturgies or any rite other than the Roman. It is not concerned with the past except when the past sheds light on the present. It does not look to the future but I could not resist a few comments here and there about what remains to be done and should be accomplished as soon as possible. What I have written is so fundamental to being a Catholic that I will be shocked if anyone finds something controversial, but I am probably a little naive about that. Frankly I will be delighted if readers conclude this trilogy with the conviction that liturgy truly is our life as Catholics.

A long time ago I learned the Latin adage, *repetitio est mater studiorum*, repetition is the mother of learning. I have found it necessary to resort to repetition of important ideas, and I trust that this will not be the father of boredom.

I mean what I have written to be like a conversation, even though a one-sided one. Liturgy is for God's people and so is this trilogy.

*"You shall make a plate of pure gold and engrave on it,
as on a seal engraving, 'Holy to the Lord.'"*
(Exodus 28:36)

Chapter 1

The Sacramental Principle

"Jesus spat on the ground, made mud with his saliva, and smeared the man's eyes with the mud." (John 9:6)

A YOUNG WOMAN TALKED her boy friend into going to Mass with her even though he was not a Catholic. He proved to be rather curious and began asking her questions. When he saw one of the ministers bring the hosts and the wine to the credence table, he asked, "What does that mean?" His girl friend told him that the bread and wine would be changed into the body and blood of Christ. Then he noticed that a server came out and lit the candles. "What does that mean?" he asked. She explained that the Mass went far back into history, long before electric lights were invented, when candles were necessary. With everything he saw, he asked, "What does that mean?" The Mass proceeded and the priest went to the ambo to preach. He took off his watch and looked at it intently. "What does that mean?" the young man asked. His girl friend replied, "Not a darn thing."

The assembly might well have expected that looking at his watch was a sign that the priest would preach briefly. Actually the liturgy is filled with signs, some of which we call sacraments. Many Catholics have learned that a sacrament is an outward sign instituted by Christ to give grace, and that there are seven sac-

1

raments. Sacraments are not ordinary signs; they effect or bring about what they signify. St. Augustine said simply that sacraments are effective signs.

The Second Vatican Council returned to a traditional understanding of sacraments which includes not only the seven liturgical rites known as sacraments but other realities of our faith. There is no single definition of a sacrament because "sacrament" is not a univocal term. It applies to many realities in different ways. And yet a synonym for "sacrament" is "mystery." A mystery is a reality beyond what can be seen, heard, and touched. This concept of sacrament indicates that the human shows forth the divine, the visible contains the invisible, and the material manifests the spiritual.

Christ himself is the most excellent of sacraments; he is the primordial sacrament; he is "the sacrament of encounter with God."[1] The Vatican Council teaches that "the Church is the universal sacrament of salvation."[2] The Council explains that "by her relationship with Christ, the Church is a kind of sacrament or sign of intimate union with God, and of the unity of all mankind. She is also an instrument for the achievement of such union and unity."[3] In a broad sense all of creation, the entire universe, can be called a sacrament in that it shows forth the wisdom and the power of God. That is why St. Paul wrote to the Romans: "Ever since the creation of the world, God's invisible attributes of eternal power and divinity have been able to be understood and perceived in what he has made."[4]

---

[1]   Such in fact is the title of the excellent book by Edward Schillebeeckx, O.P.
[2]   *Pastoral Constitution on the Church in the Modern World*, no. 45.
[3]   *Dogmatic Constitution on the Church*, no. 1.
[4]   Romans 1:20.

Sacraments are transcendent human experiences. An experience is an event which we live through, such as taking a trip to Rome. Simply day dreaming about going to Rome is not an experience. Experience includes personal involvement. The baby who sleeps through his parents' touring of Rome does not experience that city. Experience is a human function. It requires the human senses of seeing, hearing, touching, smelling, and tasting, as well as the human faculties of intellect and will. Now we add the word which makes sacraments different from other forms of experience, and that word is "transcendent." It is taken from a Latin verb which means "to climb over." In sacraments we climb over into a world beyond the realities which we can ascertain through human senses and human faculties. We step into the world of faith. This is not the fictional "stepping through the looking glass" of Lewis Carroll's imagination. It is a reality through grace, the gift of God.

Usually the word "sacrament" refers to the seven liturgical rites which are baptism, confirmation, Eucharist, holy order, matrimony, penance, and the anointing of the sick. We believe that these sacraments were instituted by Christ, but it is his mother who helps us to understand the sacramental principle which underlies them. That statement requires a little explanation which goes back to the early part of the fifth century.

At that time Nestorius, the bishop of Constantinople, rejected the idea that Mary could be called the Mother of God. He found it offensive to say that "God suffered" and so he thought it was even more objectionable to say that "God was born of a woman and nursed at her breast." Putting it as simply as I know how, he maintained that there are two separate persons in Jesus Christ, the one human and the other divine. He could accept the idea that Mary was the mother of the human

Jesus only. He believed that there are two natures in Christ (which is true) but insisted that each has its own personal manifestation (which is not true). Catholic doctrine is that there is only one person in Christ, a divine person who is the Son of God. The mystery of the incarnation is that this one divine person became human like us in all things but sin. In the Word made flesh he is the one who acts and who is acted upon. The Council of Ephesus in the year 431 condemned Nestorius and declared that Mary is rightly called "Theotokos," the God-bearer. St. Cyril of Alexandria, who was very active during the Council, wrote in a letter: "That anyone could doubt the right of the holy Virgin to be called Mother of God fills me with astonishment. Surely she must be the Mother of God since our Lord Jesus Christ is God, and she gave birth to him!"[5]

In the prayer known in Latin as the *Te Deum* in the Liturgy of the Hours, we say to Jesus, "When you became man to set us free, you did not spurn the Virgin's womb." The Son of God did not deem it improper for him to be conceived in Mary's womb and to be born into our world. He did not hesitate to embrace his own humanity and the people and world around him. He had to grow and to learn and to become an adult. He knew what it was to rejoice at a wedding feast and to weep at the tomb of his dead friend Lazarus. He valued the love of his parents and his disciples, and he endured the pain of his betrayal by Judas. He felt the warmth of the sun and the freshness of rain. He lived a true human life from the moment of his conception through his death on the cross. God did all these things?

---

[5]   See the Office of Readings for June 27.

Yes! God the Son did them.[6] Because he did, he gave a special sacredness to all of creation which already was holy since it had come from the hand of his Father. During his ministry, he followed the sacramental principle. He reached out and placed his hand on the leper, he touched the ear of the deaf man and said, "Be opened," and he made mud paste to smear on the eyes of the blind man to cure him. Were these actions necessary? No, since as God he could have cured merely by an act of his will, but since he was human he acted in a human manner.

All of this influences Catholic liturgy. It seems that an appreciation of the sacraments is in proportion to a true insight into Mary's maternity, and equally a poor understanding of Mary's role or even a refusal to acknowledge her as Mother of God results in a loss of sacramental awareness. The place of Mary leads us to an insight into the meaning of the incarnation and consequently of the sacramental principle.

Some religions advise their followers to escape as far as possible from the world around them. Even some Christian sects, especially those which boast that they are based on scripture alone, value but little, if at all, the sacraments and their ceremonies. In our liturgy we make use of water, oil, bread, wine, candles, incense, vestments, robes, statues, pictures, and music. The Second Vatican Council teaches us that "there is hardly any proper use of material things which cannot be directed toward the sanctification of people and the praise of God."[7] We embrace

---

[6] This truth is called in theology "the communication of idioms." It means that because there is only one person, Jesus Christ, who acts through two natures, one divine and one human, we rightly attribute to this one person actions which are both human (weeping at the tomb of Lazarus) and divine (raising him from the dead).

[7] *Constitution on the Sacred Liturgy*, no. 61.

all material things because of the incarnation. The Second Vatican Council declared: "By his incarnation and birth the Son of God has united himself with every human person. He worked with human hands, he thought with a human mind, he acted by human choice, and he loved with a human heart. Born of the Virgin Mary, Jesus became one of us, human like us in all things but sin. He has shown us the way, and if we follow it, life and death are made holy and take on a whole new meaning."[8] In accord with the example of Jesus, we *celebrate* our liturgy.

Pope St. Leo the Great, who died in 460, has left us a beautiful insight into the seven liturgical sacraments. He observed in a sermon on the feast of the Ascension: "Our Redeemer's visible presence has passed into the sacraments." The Pope made the point that following his ascension Christ "began to be indescribably more present in his divinity to those from whom he was further removed in his humanity."[9] In other words, Christ in his divinity is more available to us now through the sacraments than he was to the people of his day through his humanity.

Reflecting on Pope Leo's sermon makes me realize that Jesus chose to be limited by his humanity before his resurrection. He healed the ten lepers, but there were many more lepers who never had the opportunity to meet Jesus. He cured the man born blind, but there were many who remained blind because they never encountered Jesus. He fed the five thousand with the loaves and the fishes, but all the while thousands were starving in lands far beyond where Jesus walked and taught. He

---

[8] *Pastoral Constitution on the Church in the Modern World*, no. 22.
[9] See the Office of Readings for Friday of the Sixth Week of Easter.

forgave the sins of the paralytic and he restored Peter's mother-in-law to health, but these two were few among many in need. He graced the wedding of the unnamed couple at Cana but others were not so blessed.

Jesus never traveled beyond Galilee and Judea. He did not go to Antioch in Syria where his disciples came to be known as Christians and Catholics. He did not precede Paul in his missionary journeys throughout the Mediterranean world. He did not sail across the sea to Rome where Peter founded the Church and made that city its center. He did not venture across the ocean to the western hemisphere of which his contemporaries were unaware. All of this changed after Jesus' ascension into heaven. From that point on, as Pope Leo said, "he began to be indescribably more present in his divinity to those from whom he was further removed in his humanity."[10] The sacraments, in a way, became his humanity, his means for reaching out to all of humanity. The sacraments make all the difference. The Second Vatican Council teaches that now Christ acts in the sacraments.[11] In the sacrament of baptism Christ cleanses vast numbers of people of sin every year in the purifying waters of baptism. He cures their spiritual blindness and opens their eyes in faith. Throughout the whole world every Sunday he nourishes people with his body and blood which is a gift far greater than that received by the five thousand who were fed with five barley loaves and a couple of fish. Christ forgives the sins of the repentant in the sacrament of penance and he strengthens those

---

[10] *Ibid.*
[11] *Constitution on the Sacred Liturgy*, no. 7.

who are sick in the sacrament of anointing. He unites in love those who come before him in the sacrament of marriage.

Pope John Paul II expressed it this way: "The sacraments make the gospel live again in us, that is to say, by them the figure, the life, the mysteries, the word, the events of Jesus' life are brought into our own lives and become part of our own being."[12]

Sacraments Are Acts of Worship

I have referred to the seven "liturgical" sacraments. That adjective not only sets apart these seven rites from all other forms of sacraments but also indicates their special character as acts of worship. In treating the liturgical sacraments, the *Constitution on the Sacred Liturgy* states that "the purpose of the sacraments is to sanctify people, to build up the body of Christ, and finally to give worship to God."[13] This statement includes the idea that the sacraments were instituted to give grace, that is, they are for the sanctification of people. The *Constitution* goes further to show that the sacraments are also for the building up of the Church, and most importantly of all, they are a means to give worship to God. In other words, every sacrament says something specific about those who celebrate the sacrament, about the Church as a whole, and about the glory of God. Still further since the grace of all the sacraments is derived from Christ's paschal mystery, the six sacraments flow from and lead to the sacrament of the Eucharist, which is the sacrament of the paschal mystery.

---

[12] From the Pope's homily at a Confirmation in Turin, September 2, 1988.
[13] *Constitution on the Sacred Liturgy*, no. 59.

An easy example is the sacrament of marriage. Marriage unites a man and a woman so that they are no longer two but one flesh in a union which is fruitful in offspring. They bear witness to the truth that the union between Christ and his Church is like their marital union and is fruitful in those who are born of water and the Holy Spirit in baptism. As an act of worship marriage shows God's wonderful attribute of love. Those are the three aspects of the sacrament of marriage: union of a man and woman which is fruitful in offspring, a witness to the union of Christ and his Church and their spiritual offspring, and the proclamation that God is a God of love. In the Eucharist married couples find both the source and the example of their love since in the Eucharist is celebrated the event to which Jesus referred when he said at the Last Supper, "There is no greater love than to lay down one's life for one's friends."[14]

All sacraments have three effects and center on the Eucharist. The sacrament of penance forgives sin, restores the penitent to full union with the Church, and proclaims that God is a God of forgiveness. This sacrament clears the way for the full celebration of the Eucharist. The sacrament of anointing helps to overcome illness, gives strength for the person to return to an active life in the Church, and shows that God is a God of healing. God's ultimate act of healing we will experience in the resurrection, which is the promise offered to us in the Eucharist.

The sacraments of initiation which are baptism, confirmation, and first Eucharist, center on the gift of life, everlasting life, the life of God within us. They grant life to people to make

---

[14] John 15:13.

them children of God, bring them into union with the whole Church, and proclaim that God is life. Baptism empowers us to celebrate the Eucharist and confirmation moves us to draw others to the Eucharist. Ordination makes a person a priest, entrusts him with the reconciliation of people with God through the ministry of the Church, and proclaims that God is our Redeemer through his incarnate Son. A priest is the sacramental person in the Church, and his ministry reaches its zenith in the sacrament of the Eucharist.

The most important aspect of sacraments, and perhaps the least emphasized, is the specifically liturgical aspect, which is the worship of God. The seven sacraments worship God as he is the God of life, of redemption, of love, of forgiveness, and of healing. The God of these attributes is indeed worthy of the greatest worship we can offer him.

Next we consider in some detail the sacraments of initiation or identity. They answer the question, who are we in the Church?

Chapter 2

Sacraments of Initiation

"Go and make disciples of all the nations; baptize them in the
name of the Father and of the Son and of the Holy Spirit."
(Matthew 28:19)

Aɴ ᴇʟᴅᴇʀʟʏ ɴᴜɴ ʜᴀᴅ ʙᴇᴇɴ a devoted fan of the New Orleans
Saints from the day they entered the National Football League.
Every Sunday she sat in front of the TV with her rosary and
prayed for the Saints, but the team never won a single playoff
game. The nun died and went directly to heaven. After a short
while, she told St. Peter that she was very happy in heaven but
she would like to know what hell was like. In an instant she was
in the lower regions. The door to hell opened and to her great
shock she saw nothing but ice. Everything was frozen over. "Take
me back," she said to St. Peter. Upon arriving in heaven, she
said, "St. Peter, I don't understand — all that cold in hell?" St.
Peter said, "Sister, I forgot to tell you. After you died, the New
Orleans Saints won the Super Bowl."[1]

The existence of hell is a Catholic doctrine, but many theologians like to point out that God does not condemn people to

---

[1] For this story I am indebted to my brother, Clarence Miller, a native and resi-
dent of New Orleans.

hell; they choose it for themselves. The first psalm says, "The Lord guides the way of the just," but then it adds, "The way of the wicked leads to doom." The wicked choose hell but we do not earn heaven for having been good. Heaven is our inheritance as the children of God. St. Paul reminds us that "The Spirit bears witness with our spirit that we are children of God, and if children, then heirs, heirs of God and joint heirs with Christ."[2]

We become God's children through the sacraments of Christian initiation. They are baptism, confirmation, and First Eucharist. Frankly I am not particularly fond of the term "initiation." It suggests that we are enduring some trial in order to join a fraternity or a sorority. I respect the term and use it because it is widely accepted, but I much prefer the term "sacraments of conformity," or even better, "sacraments of identity." Baptism, confirmation, and first Eucharist are the sacraments by which we are conformed to the image of God's Son so that he might be the first-born of many brothers and sisters.[3] They are the sacraments which give us our identity in the family of the Church. What's in a name? That which we call the sacraments of initiation by any other name still are the means by which, with all sins forgiven, we share the image of God's Son and become children of God, brothers and sisters of one another, people of the Church, sharers in the royal priesthood of Christ, and heirs of heaven. Is there a name good enough to be applied to all of that?

---

[2] Romans 8:16-17. See also Ephesians 1:14.
[3] See Romans 8:29.

Baptism and the Paschal Mystery

Baptism is our initial sharing in the paschal mystery of Christ, a truth which St. Paul emphasized in his Letter to the Romans. He wrote, "Are you unaware that we who were baptized into Christ Jesus were baptized into his death? We were indeed buried with him through baptism into death so that, just as Christ was raised from the dead by the glory of the Father, we too might live in newness of life."[4] Paul did not preach to the Romans; they were not his converts. He asks, "Are you unaware" of the meaning of baptism. He seems to imply, "Surely your preachers stressed this great truth for you." And a great truth it is.

Paul seems to envision that the sign of death and burial with Christ is baptism by immersion. Coming up from the water is then a sign of resurrection. Actually water in itself is both a sign of death and a sign of life. Anyone upon a lake in a tempest, even seasoned fishermen, fear death by drowning, and yet we all know that water is necessary for life. In baptism water becomes a transcendent human experience. It brings us into contact with the paschal mystery through which Christ by dying destroyed our death and by rising restored our life.

There is another level of meaning in baptism, and it is the truth that baptism is conformity to Christ who is the death-resurrection person. That is his identity as the Son of God in the flesh. When Jesus died on the cross, he offered his life to the Father. He cried out, "Into your hands I commend my spirit." He gave his life to God to acknowledge that his life had come

---

[4] Romans 6:3-4.

from God. The person from whom one receives life is that person's father. So it is that Jesus by the act of dying proclaimed the truth which he had declared in words during his ministry, that God is really his Father. In the resurrection God restored life to his Son to show that he truly is the life-giver, that he is Jesus' Father. The paschal mystery is an expression in time and space of the reality of the Trinity in eternity. In eternity the Father begets his Son and the Son responds in love to his Father. The paschal mystery is the transcendent human experience of that divine, eternal reality. Baptism for us, then, is a conformity to Christ who is the death-resurrection person.

I am firmly convinced of the importance of this theology but I must confess I have a hard time making it clear. I will try again. Sometimes a lover says, "I would give my life for you." Jesus did not give his life *for* his Father but *to* his Father. Through his dying Jesus said by action what he had said by words, "God is my Father." When Jesus was baptized in the Jordan, God said to him, "You are my beloved Son." When Jesus was transfigured on the mountain, God said, "This is my Son, my beloved."[5] When God raised Jesus from the dead, he announced by action what he had said by words, "Jesus is my Son." Being the Son of God is Jesus' identity. That identity was proclaimed in the paschal mystery. We enter into the paschal mystery by means of baptism so that we may become conformed to Jesus as the Son of God. Jesus is the death-resurrection person; the paschal mystery expresses his identity.

We celebrate the paschal mystery in every Eucharist and in a special way throughout the sacred triduum. The American bishops have told us that "Christian spirituality consists in the

---

[5] See Mark 1:11 and 9:7.

living out in experience, throughout the whole course of our lives, of the death-resurrection of Christ that we have been caught up into by baptism."[6] Our final participation in the paschal mystery comes with our death and subsequently with the day of resurrection.

Water is the essential sign of baptism. Very important too is the white garment, the sign that we have been cleansed from sin and that we have "put on" Christ, that we have become a person in the Church, a member of Christ's body. [Never should the white garment be treated as optional!][7] This is the garment which is the proper robe for all liturgical ministers, a sign that they carry out a truly liturgical function because through baptism they have become sharers in the royal priesthood of Christ. Next is the candle, the sign of faith, which enlightens us and which enlightens everyone to whom we offer the witness of faith.

When infants are baptized, the priest says to the participants: "These children have been reborn in baptism. They are now called children of God, for so indeed they are. They will call God their Father in the midst of the church." Then as a climax to the ceremony all present say the "Our Father" in the name of the newly baptized. Adults in the catechumenate during Lent are presented with a copy of this prayer as a gift from God and his Church. Following their baptism and confirmation when they take part in their first celebration of the Eucharist they will say it together with the rest of the baptized, the daughters and sons of God and their sisters and brothers in the family of God.

---

[6] *Spiritual Renewal of the American Priesthood*, p. 3.
[7] That the ritual allows the ceremony with the white garment to be omitted is a grave error in judgment.

The Sacrament of Confirmation

The anointing at the conclusion of baptism may be seen as an expression of Christ as Priest, Prophet, and King, but actually it anticipates the anointing of confirmation (and it is omitted when confirmation immediately follows baptism). Confirmation does not stand on its own; it flows from and completes baptism. Pope Paul VI in 1971 in his *Apostolic Constitution on the Sacrament of Confirmation* gives some clarity to this frequently misinterpreted sacrament. I think I can do well by quoting directly from his *Constitution*:

"The apostles, in fulfillment of Christ's wish, imparted the gift of the Spirit to the newly baptized by the laying on of hands to complete the grace of baptism. — Confirmation in a certain way perpetuates the grace of Pentecost in the Church. This makes clear the specific importance of confirmation for sacramental initiation by which the faithful as members of the living Christ are incorporated into him and made like him through baptism and through confirmation and the Eucharist. — Through the sacrament of confirmation those who have been born anew in baptism receive the inexpressible Gift, the Holy Spirit himself, by which they are endowed with special strength. Having received the character of this sacrament, they are bound more intimately to the Church and they are more strictly obliged to spread and defend the faith both by word and by deed as true witnesses of Christ. Finally, confirmation is so closely linked with the holy Eucharist that the faithful, after being signed by holy baptism and confirmation, are incorporated fully into the body of Christ by participation in the Eucharist."

The Pope decreed that "the sacrament of confirmation is conferred through the anointing with chrism on the forehead, which is done by the laying on of the hand, and through the words, 'Be sealed with the gift of the Holy Spirit.'" The word "sealed" comes from Paul's Letter to the Ephesians: "You were sealed with the Holy Spirit who had been promised."[8] This word in Greek, *sphragis*, referred to the mark placed upon a document or letter to guarantee its genuineness or authenticity. Such documents were closed with molten wax into which was pressed the distinctive seal of the sender. The Holy Spirit with whom we are sealed confirms that we belong to God.

Baptism leads directly to the celebration of the Eucharist; confirmation too is closely related to the Eucharist. We quite rightly think of confirmation as a sacrament of service in the family of the Church, a sacrament of the apostolate. To show the relationship of confirmation to the Eucharist, the Council teaches that "the goal of apostolic works is that all who are made children of God by faith and baptism should come together to praise God in the midst of his Church, to take part in her sacrifice, and to eat the Lord's supper."[9]

As Pentecost completes the paschal mystery, so confirmation completes baptism. Underlying the entire *Constitution* by Pope Paul VI is the truth that baptism and confirmation are intimately connected and that the proper order of sacraments requires that confirmation be received before First Eucharist. That proper order suffered from an historical mistake. I can exemplify what happened from the life of my mother. My mother was born in 1892. She was baptized as an infant that same year. She was confirmed in 1904 at the age of twelve and she received her First Holy Communion two years later at the

---

[8] Ephesians 1:13.
[9] *Constitution on the Sacred Liturgy*, no. 10.

age of fourteen. That was normal. Even though confirmation had become separated from baptism, the proper order of sacraments had been maintained. Then in 1910 Pope Pius X decided that it was not proper to keep little children from Holy Communion, and so he lowered the age for First Communion to seven. The Pope made an admirable pastoral decision regarding First Communion, but he failed to lower the age of confirmation so that it could be received before First Eucharist. That is how for the first time in history, the order of sacraments had become inverted. In 1930 the Congregation of Rites, which at the time was in charge of the sacraments, announced that the proper order of sacraments should be restored, but no one seemed sure of the best way to achieve that goal and nothing was done. Then imaginative people went to work and created a new theology for confirmation. They began to teach that confirmation is a sacrament of maturity, a growing-up sacrament, a rite of passage. That approach is not in accord with the traditional understanding of confirmation.

Writing in the seventeenth century, St. John Eudes succinctly expressed the tradition of the Church: "This great gift (conformity to Christ) originates from baptism. It is increased and strengthened through confirmation and by making good use of other graces that are given by God. Through the holy Eucharist it is brought to perfection."[10]

Quite properly the Rite of Christian Initiation of Adults has returned to the traditional order of sacraments and the intimate connection between baptism and confirmation. The bishops of the United States still must come to a decision regarding

---

[10] From his *Treatise on the Admirable Heart of Jesus*, quoted in the Office of Readings for August 19.

those who are baptized as infants. In some dioceses we continue to live under the anomaly that the proper order of sacraments must be maintained for adults but not for those baptized as infants. The principles are clear: baptism and confirmation should not be separated and both should precede First Eucharist. The bishops do not seem to agree on a solution. Since we sense that we need some religious experience for youth to make their passage into maturity, the bishops should create such a ceremony, a kind of Catholic bar mitzvah, of course for both girls and boys, and not try to change a sacrament from its original meaning to fit a current need.

Meanwhile we need to appreciate the truth that through baptism and confirmation we become persons in the Church. These are sacraments of identity. They conform us to Christ. They make us children of God as Jesus is the Son of God. We fulfill these sacraments by following the commandment of Jesus, "Become like little children." These sacraments are the source of our dignity and our worth. We saw in Chapter 3 of Book 1 that little children are precious to their parents because of who they are, not because of what they accomplish. Rather what they accomplish has value in the eyes of their parents because of who they are as their children. Good parents love their children more than children love their parents, and God our Father loves us far beyond our powers to realize or to reciprocate.

The Eucharist As Identity

Baptism and confirmation fulfill the teaching of the Council: "It has pleased God to save us and to make us holy, not merely as individuals without any mutual bonds, but by forming us into a single people, a people who worship him in truth (baptism) and who serve him in holiness (confirmation)." Our First Communion both celebrates our Christian initiation and increases our conformity to Christ. This First Communion, and each one that follows, is a sacrament of growth in Christ. Through the Eucharist we can gradually become more and more like Christ.

To become more like Christ was the aspiration of a French priest who was canonized by Pope John Paul II on Trinity Sunday, June 2, 1996. John Gabriel Perboyre was a Vincentian who yearned to go as a missionary to China but like many Vincentians before and after him, he was assigned to seminary work. With a persistence which in saints is called perseverance and in the rest of us is called stubbornness, he prevailed upon his superior who at last sent him to China. After learning the rudiments of the language, which he found to be very difficult, he proved successful in winning converts until a terrible persecution broke out. He was betrayed to the Chinese officials by one of his own converts, and he was arrested and imprisoned. After being dragged from one tribunal to another, he was at last led out to a hill where on a Friday afternoon he was strangled to death while hanging from a cross. Pope Leo XIII, who beatified John Gabriel, commented on the remarkable similarity between the suffering and death of Jesus and that of the Vincentian priest. A beautiful prayer is attributed to John Gabriel which expresses his spirituality. This is that prayer:

> "O my divine Savior, transform me into yourself. May my hands be the hands of Jesus. May my tongue be the tongue of Jesus. Grant that every faculty of my body may serve only to glorify you. Above all, trans-

form my soul and all its powers that my memory, my will, and my affections may be the memory, the will, and the affections of Jesus. I pray you to destroy in me all that is not of you. Grant that I may live but in you and by you and for you, and that I may truly say with St. Paul, 'I live, now not I, but Christ lives in me.'"

I can find no evidence that John Gabriel ever read St. John Eudes, but that saint beautifully expressed the same Christian ideal in his *Treatise on the Admirable Heart of Jesus*: "Jesus desires that whatever is in him may live and rule in you: his breath in your breath, his heart in your heart, all the faculties of his soul are the faculties of your soul, so that these words may be fulfilled in you: 'Glorify God and bear him in your body, that the life of Jesus may be made manifest in you.'"[11] I believe that it is very appropriate to say the prayer of St. John Gabriel silently after Holy Communion.

We are privileged to receive communion during every Mass, but baptism and confirmation may be received only once. They may not be repeated because they give us our Christian identity. They are sacraments of conformity to Christ. The analogy is that they imprint an indelible character on the soul.

One other sacrament may be received only once. It too can be said to imprint an indelible character since it too is a sacrament of conformity to Christ, a sacrament of identity. It is the sacrament of ordination. This chapter is not complete without it since it belongs with a treatment on baptism and confirmation.

---

[11] *Ibid.* The scripture which he quotes is 1 Corinthians 6:20.

The Sacrament of Ordination

A priest was celebrating his golden jubilee of ordination. During a simple dinner which some of his close friends had given for him, he reflected on the length of his service and of how grateful he was that he had been granted the privilege of being a priest for fifty years. Then he added in a melancholy tone, "But, you know, I am a little relieved that my time as a priest is coming to an end, rather than beginning, because I am no longer quite sure what a priest is."

I was not shocked by his statement but I was moved to reflect on my years as a priest and of how different things are now from that day when I was ordained in 1956. I have heard some priests complain that, because of the emphasis on the laity in the Church, there has been a blurring of the distinction between the priesthood of the ordained and that of the baptized. Others have wondered why they should bother when lay people, not to mention deacons, can do so many things which used to be reserved to priests.

One could, and perhaps should, admit that there really is little difference between priests and lay people, even though that difference is in essence and not merely in degree. We all share the call to holiness, which means to become like Christ, to become conformed to his image. The Christian vocation for everyone is clearly expressed by St. Paul in his Letter to the Romans: "Those whom God foreknew he predestined to be conformed to the image of his Son so that the Son might be the firstborn of many brothers and sisters."[12] That is why the prayer

---

[12] Romans 8:29.

of St. John Gabriel Perboyre is appropriate for all of us and not just for priests.

We may rightly ask whether there is a distinctive holiness and purpose for a priest. I can suggest a theology which by no means is a defined dogma of the Church, but which makes sense to me and puts not only the identity but the role of the ordained priest into perspective.

The incarnation of the Son of God came about because of sin. The love of God was so great that he would not allow sin to frustrate his plan for his people.[13] Jesus was born to be our savior, to be the Lamb of God who takes away the sins of the world. Some theologians, generally Franciscans, say that even if we had never sinned the Son would have become human so that God the Father might manifest his great love for us. It is a nice thought, but who knows? Other theologians, mostly Dominicans, point out that it is hard enough trying to figure out what God has done in accord with our condition without worrying about what he would have done in a condition which does not exist. Our faith is that for us and for our salvation the Son of God became human. He came to destroy sin. In becoming human the Son of God became our priest. Negative though it may sound, priesthood is concerned with sin. Without sin, one can suppose, there would have been no need for priesthood because there would have been no need for a mediator and a savior.

Sin separates. It divides. It disintegrates. It works a division inside us. We are torn in tension between good and evil within ourselves. Sin leads us into slavery. We do not do the

---

[13] See Ephesians 1:3-14.

good we will to do, but the evil we do not intend.[14] Sin also separates us from our fellow human beings. Sin forced a wedge between Adam and his wife Eve, and it moved Cain to murder his brother Abel. Above all sin separates us from God.

Jesus entered the breach. He came to draw all things to himself in unity, to restore wholeness to creation, to give us harmony within ourselves, and to solidify us in our relationship with God and each other. The mission of Jesus was reconciliation. Sin separates and divides; reconciliation unites. Jesus' mission was to bring about unity in love and peace. He prayed for that unity at the Last Supper: "Father, that they all may be one, as we are one." And for that unity he died on Good Friday. But before he was lifted up from the earth to draw all things to himself, he gave us the holy Eucharist as the sacrament of reconciliation and unity.

What I suggest is that baptism-confirmation is a conformity to Christ as he is the eternal Son of God. Ordination is conformity to Christ as he is human, for it is in his humanity that Christ is our priest, our reconciler. (This is not to suggest that ordination conforms one to Christ is his maleness. Ordination effects an incarnational conformity, not a sexual one.) What follows from this theology is the truth that the unique work of the priest is reconciliation.[15] He is to lead people to the freedom of the children of God so that they are not slaves to sin. He must bring together people who, if left to themselves, would remain separated from each other by sin. He is to form the Christian community by word and sacrament. He is called "Fa-

---

[14] So says St. Paul in Romans 7:19.

[15] The episcopal motto of Cardinal Roger Mahony, Archbishop of Los Angeles, is "To Reconcile God's People."

ther" because he brings people back from the separateness of sin into the family of God in the Church.

Through the sacraments of Christian initiation the priest introduces people into the Church. He makes them part of the family. Wounded by sin, every person is like the man on the road from Jerusalem to Jericho who fell prey to robbers who stripped him, beat him, and left him half dead. That is what sin has done to us all. In baptism-confirmation Christ heals our wounds and brings us to the inn, the Church, where we await his return. We are born again as sisters and brothers of Christ, sons and daughters of the same Father in the family of the Church. We become part of the household.

Of this family of the Church, Christian marriage is a symbol. It is part of personal reconciliation, a means to overcome the separation of sex from love, and it is a sign of social reconciliation, our oneness in the love of Christ. Priests stand before the celebrants of the sacrament of marriage as a reminder that Christian marriage is an image of the union of Christ and his Church.

Sickness separates a person from service to the community. When you are sick, you have to take care of yourself; you have to leave off your usual occupations and turn inward. Priests anoint people to strengthen them to join their sufferings to those of Christ and his body, the Church, and, if God wishes, to restore them to full active participation in the community of the Church.

More serious than physical illness is sin, which is spiritual sickness. Sin is the disease of the mystical body. It disintegrates. It is an obstacle to the effect of the Eucharist. The sacrament of penance clears the way for reconciliation with God and his people and leads to the Eucharist. Penance does not stand alone.

It is related to the Eucharist as a means to the end. Penance is a sacrament *for* reconciliation. The Eucharist is the sacrament *of* reconciliation. (This truth is beautifully illustrated by the two Eucharistic Prayers for Masses of Reconciliation.) In the Church we are a pilgrim people, a people on a journey. The man in the parable of the Good Samaritan was going the wrong way. He was going down from Jerusalem to Jericho. But all through the gospel Luke presents Jesus as going up to Jerusalem. It was there that he would offer the sacrifice of himself to the Father for the reconciliation of the world. The Eucharist is the sacrament of going up to Jerusalem with Christ, to share in his sacrifice which destroys sins and restores unity. The Eucharist, the summit of all the sacraments and of priestly ministry, is indeed the great sacrament of reconciliation.

The funeral Mass on August 27, 1988 for Art Rooney, the highly respected owner of the Pittsburgh Steelers, was attended by football people from across the nation. When Bishop Donald Wuerl, in preparation for communion, said, "Let us offer each other a sign of peace," the commissioner of the National Football League, Pete Rozelle, tapped the shoulder of the man in front of him, the Oakland Raiders owner, Al Davis. The two longtime adversaries shook hands. It was a small gesture, perhaps only a beginning of reconciliation, but the power of the Eucharist was evident.

The role of the priest, through word and sacrament, is to make people aware that the Church is God's family on pilgrimage, united by Christ, that we need to be concerned about each other, that we must form a community not only in being but in prayer and action. The mother of Jesus is a model for the role of a priest. The Preface for the Mass in honor of Mary, Image and Mother of the Church, says of Mary: "She joined her prayers with those of the apostles, as together they awaited the coming of your Spirit, and so became the perfect pattern of the Church at prayer."[16] The Church is important to us not only because it is the way to heaven but because it is the right way to live together on our way to heaven. There is no room for rugged individualism or smug narcissism in the Church. There should be no tolerance for anything which separates and divides us from each other. We must overcome anything which vitiates the purpose of the sacrificial death of Jesus.

As Jesus hung upon the cross, he seemed to be all alone, but he was drawing all of humanity to himself to win for his Father a holy people. As we saw in Chapter 4 of Book 2, the presider's chair at Mass is an important symbol. This chair should stand alone; it is not to be flanked by other chairs. The reason is that the presider, bishop or priest, is the sacrament of Christ the priest who is the reconciler, the former of community. Everyone is not a priest even though every baptized person shares in the universal priesthood of Christ. There is one chair to show that there is one priest who acts in the person of Christ to make us all one in Christ.

The Council forcefully opposed individualism and clearly taught that we are to move together, and not alone, on the journey toward our destiny in Christ. The kind of spirituality which a priest is to teach and exemplify is Church spirituality which overcomes divisions and brings people together. It is sacramental spirituality, and the priest is the sacramental person of the Church. All the sacraments are for reconciliation, for drawing us from the disintegration of sin into the unity of the Church. The ultimate sacrament of reconciliation is the Eucharist.

---

[16] The allusion is to Acts 1:14.

The great tragedy of our era is that liturgy, which is the means to unity, has been made into an arena of division within the Church. Evil is at work to vitiate the promotion and restoration of the liturgy which the *Constitution on the Sacred Liturgy* states is "rightly held to be a sign of the providential dispositions of God in our time, as a movement of the Holy Spirit in his Church."[17] Priests must in conscience see to the full and proper implementation of all the liturgical norms of the Church, extremists in either direction to the contrary notwithstanding. Without the liturgy priests have no purpose.

Priests must make their own the words of Paul: "The love of Christ impels us who have reached the conviction that since one died for all, all died. He died for all... so that we might live no longer for ourselves but for him.... All this has been done by God who has reconciled us to himself through Christ and has given us the ministry of reconciliation."[18] Priests, like Jesus in his humanity, have been given the ministry of reconciliation in the Church. Reconciliation is not only a sacramental role for priests. It is a way of life, a way of being Christ to the people of the Church. That is the meaning of the sacrament of ordination.

Sometimes a spirit of reconciliation can go too far. An elderly priest was renowned as a marriage counselor, even though he always insisted on seeing husband and wife separately. A newly ordained priest assigned as his associate decided he would learn from his pastor by eavesdropping on one of his counseling sessions. The wife entered first, sat down, and immediately said, "Father, my husband does not appreciate me. I try to make

---

[17] *Constitution on the Sacred Liturgy*, no. 43.
[18] 2 Corinthians 5:14ff.

everything nice for him. I keep a clean house and cook him good meals, but he never wants to take me anywhere. All he wants to do is watch TV and drink beer. I think I deserve better than that." The old priest patted her hand and said, "You are so right. You are so right." With that she left and her husband came and sat down and immediately said, "Father my wife does not appreciate me. I work hard and earn a good living for us. She can go out and buy nice clothes and never has to worry about anything, but all she does is complain about me. I think I deserve better than that." The old priest shook the man's hand and said, "You are so right. You are so right." With that the husband left and the young priest came in. He said, "Father, this is terrible. Here you agree with both of these people which does them no good. Besides you should see them together." The old priest sighed and said, "You are so right. You are so right."

The Bishop of the Diocese

I would indeed be remiss if in a treatment of the sacrament of ordination I were to neglect the bishop who in his ordination receives the fullness of the priesthood. Although the bishop is chosen and appointed by the Pope, he receives his authority as shepherd of his diocese directly from Christ. His authority flows immediately from his office. He has what is called in canonical language "ordinary power." In the 1917 *Code of Canon Law* the diocesan bishop was known as the Ordinary. This word is derived from the Latin for "overseer." It is also related to the name of the sacrament which the bishop has received in full, and in which priests and deacons share, "holy order."

The diocesan bishop oversees, or presides over, the entire

diocese entrusted to him. He is its chief shepherd and primary teacher, and all deacons, priests, and auxiliary bishops receive their jurisdiction from him. They extend his pastoral office to the parishes and other parts of the diocese.

I have actually heard some Catholics say, "Don't tell me what the bishop says. I want to know what the Pope says. I follow the Pope, not any bishop." Be assured that the first person to condemn this attitude is the Pope himself. Accepting the Pope but not the bishop is like saying, "I recognize the President of the United States but not the Governor of my state."

Two persons living on this earth are mentioned by name in every eucharistic prayer. They are the Pope and the diocesan bishop. We name them, not primarily to pray for them (even though they need our prayers because of the burdens of their office), but to express our unity with them. As no legitimate celebration of the Eucharist can take place except in union with the Pope, so in the diocese no legitimate celebration of the Eucharist can take place except in union with the bishop.

Unity is so important in the Catholic Church that it is essential for us to embrace the diocesan bishop as the one pastor of the entire diocese. We are a people of one Lord, one faith, and one baptism. There is but one God and Father of us all. As the Pope is the minister of unity for the universal Church, so the diocesan bishop is the minister of unity for the diocese.

When priests extend the bishop to all parts and people of his diocese, they share in his prophetic and priestly office. Their primary role is preaching and the liturgy. Deacons through their ordination share in the apostolic role of the bishop. Their primary role is one of charity and administration. But there is only one sacrament of holy order, or ordination, which is shared in three ways by bishops, priests, and deacons.

The Rite of Christian Initiation of Adults

I debated with myself whether I should write to any extensive degree on the RCIA, and I decided that, because there are many current and excellent treatments, only a few comments were sufficient for this book. The first point is that the Rite is basically a restoration and not an innovation. Until the edict of Milan in the year 313, which granted toleration and even positive encouragement as a civic virtue to everyone to practice the religion of their choice, it was both special and dangerous to be a Catholic. It was special because adults at least were expected to make a conscious and deliberate choice to become a Catholic, and it was dangerous because the extent and fury of persecution meant that it was precarious to be a Catholic, as the large number of martyrs attests. The Church rose to prominence after the Emperor Constantine was baptized on his death bed, and when his sons began a trend to suppress paganism. The result was not only freedom for the Church, but ease about becoming a Catholic, and even an expectation that one would join the Church. The original form of what we call the RCIA died out.

The Second Vatican Council decreed that the catechumenate for adults was to be restored.[19] I wish to observe only two points about the restored rite. The first is that it is not a program of instruction. Although it includes instruction, it is primarily a liturgical rite of prayer and formation over a period of time, perhaps even for two years. It is, and should be treated as, part of the entire rite of baptism, confirmation, and First Eucharist, the three sacraments of Christian initiation. Baptism

---

[19] *Constitution on the Sacred Liturgy*, no. 64.

does not begin during the ceremonies of the Easter Vigil but with this rite.

The second point is that the rite is not exclusively a clerical domain but a cooperative effort of the team of lay people, sometimes also religious, with the priest. It reflects the truth that Christ shares his priesthood in two ways, with the baptized and with the ordained, but that there is only one priest in the Catholic Church.

The RCIA, I must observe, is an important advance over the six instructions which a priest customarily offered to converts before their baptism or their admission into the Church. The RCIA is another example of how the liturgy and the life of the Church have been uplifted by the action of the Holy Spirit in the Second Vatican Council.

Summary

Baptism and confirmation enable the people of the Church to participate in the sacraments of the Eucharist, marriage, penance, and the anointing of the sick. For Eucharist, penance and anointing the priest is the presider, and for marriage he is the witness. The three sacraments of marriage, penance, and anointing are topics for the next two chapters.

Chapter 3

The Sacrament of Marriage

"This is a great foreshadowing; I mean that it refers to Christ and his Church." (Ephesians 5:32)

A YOUNG WOMAN SAID to her mother, "Mother dear, I cannot marry Harold, even though he is fabulously wealthy." Her mother asked, "Daughter dear, why cannot you marry Harold, even though he is fabulously wealthy?" "Because, mother dear," she responded, "he does not believe in hell, and I cannot convince him." Her mother said, "You marry him and I'll convince him."

I apologize for continuing the negative image of a mother-in-law, but I could not resist telling that story. In reparation I recommend a reading of the Book of Ruth in the Bible which tells of the beautiful relationship between Ruth and her mother-in-law, Naomi. The biblical author was interested in Ruth because she became an ancestress of King David, but the narrative helps us to reflect that although marriage is between one man and one woman, it necessarily goes beyond the relationship of only two people. A connection with others, a linking together, is part of marriage. In most instances marriage is fruitful in offspring. Children are related to their parents and to each other. More people enter into the relationships. They are called, quite appropriately, relatives: uncles, aunts, cousins, and in-laws. (I devoutly wish we could find another term for "in-laws," since it sounds legalistic.) There is a further type of relationship: when people adopt children, they reflect the action of God toward us as expressed by St. Paul: "You did not receive a spirit of slavery leading you back into fear, but a spirit of adoption through which we cry out, 'Abba,' Father."[1] Godparents at baptism are of profound significance as the name suggests. Friends of the family are part of the picture. In fact, all of these relationships are a portrait of the Church: many people related through Christ who are called to live in love and harmony.

St. Paul writes of marriage, "This is a great foreshadowing; I mean that it refers to Christ and the Church."[2] Christian marriage is a sign, a sacrament, of the intimate relationship of love between Christ and all the many people of his Church.

The first place in the sacrament of marriage belongs to God. Since the sacrament is liturgical, it is an expression of worship. It acknowledges that our God is a God of love. It does so not only through prayers during the ceremony but directly by the act of consent through which a man and a woman are joined as husband and wife. For people of faith, that act says, "We profess that our love comes from God since God is love."

Of all the billions of couples who have been joined in marriage throughout history, one couple was especially favored, a couple whose marriage has become immortal even though they remain unnamed. They are the couple who celebrated their wedding at Cana in Galilee and who had Jesus as their guest. By his presence he showed his approval of their marriage and

---

[1] Romans 8:15.
[2] Ephesians 5:32.

blessed their union. He even gave them a wedding present, a very extraordinary gift, the miracle of changing water into wine.

But no man and woman who are joined in the sacrament of marriage need to envy that young couple at Cana. Jesus is not the guest of couples today, it is true; rather they are his guest. He invites them into his home, the church, and calls them to the most intimate part of his home near the altar. He does more than approve of their marriage. He himself is the bond of love which unites them together. At they stand hand in hand, his grace flows from one to the other, joining them as husband and wife. He even gives them a wedding present, an extraordinary gift, not water changed into wine, but bread and wine changed into his body and blood. He gives that gift not only once but every time a couple chooses to come to the altar to receive him in Holy Communion.

Mary at Cana was eager that everything would go right for the couple during both their marriage and the wedding banquet. We see how solicitous she was since she was the one who noticed that the wine had run out. As the model and exemplar of the Church, Mary shows us that the whole Church is eager that marriage be celebrated properly and that the Eucharist be the source of joy and jubilation as was the wine at Cana. In particular Mary's role is fulfilled by parents, relatives, and friends, by the wedding coordinator of the parish, by those who participated in an engaged encounter or similar experience with the couple, by those in the wedding party, by the musicians, and by all those who worked with and for the couple so that their wedding day could be an event of lasting happiness. Oh, I almost forgot: the priest has a role too as the witness of the Church. Bishop Fulton Sheen wrote a beautiful book called

Three To Get Married. The third party is, of course, God. Actually it takes a lot of people for two to get married.

It is most appropriate that Catholic couples be married within Mass, not only so that they may receive Holy Communion, but also because the Mass makes present for them on the altar the greatest act of love the world has even seen, the sacrificial death of Jesus. We need to reject weak excuses for not having a Mass, such as many of those present are not Catholic (it will be edifying for them to witness a Mass) or the Mass makes the ceremony too long (not nearly as long as the reception afterwards).

These days the priest is to invite the couple to select appropriate scripture readings for the wedding Mass. Frequently they choose the beautiful reading on love from the thirteenth chapter of St. Paul's First Epistle to the Corinthians. That passage contains a practical list of love's characteristics: "Love is patient, love is kind, love is not self-seeking, love never fails." It is a good idea for couples at least once a year on their anniversary to read that chapter aloud to each other. As they reflect on how they have not always fulfilled the ideal presented by St. Paul, they should not be discouraged but should deepen a conviction that the ideal of true love is found in the Eucharist and that in receiving communion together they can receive the grace they need to grow toward fulfilling that ideal.

These are the three aspects of the sacrament of marriage: the union of a man and woman which is fruitful in offspring, a witness to the union of Christ and the people of his Church, and the proclamation that God is a God of love.

Chapter 4

The Sacraments of Penance and Anointing and Funerals

PENANCE

"Whose sins you shall forgive, they are forgiven." (John 20:23)

REMEMBER THE ELDERLY NUN in a previous chapter who was a big fan of the New Orleans Saints? Even in her old age she was still teaching in the parochial school. She had the practice of going to confession once a week. She and the other sisters were blessed because the priest came over to the convent every Saturday morning for confessions, but one Saturday he called to say he just could not make it. The old nun was undaunted. That night she did what she had never done before, she went to the parish church for confession. She stood in line and when her turn came she entered the very dark, old fashioned confessional. She became confused, missed the kneeler, and fell backwards into the aisle, making a terrible racket. A gentleman helped her to her feet, and she tried again. This time she fell against the wall of the confessional and made still further noise. The slide opened and she said, "Bless me, Father for I have sinned. My main sin is that I am so impatient with all my children." The priest asked, "How many children do you have?" She answered,

"Forty-five." The priest said, "Get out of here, woman. I knew you were drunk when you came in."

Confession under those circumstances seems to be just about the most private and individual religious experience a person can have, and yet the Council teaches that this sacrament is liturgical. It is part of the public worship of the Church regarding which the Council insists that "the aim to be considered above all else is the full, active participation by all the faithful."[1] People and priest come together for penance, just as they do for the other sacraments. [By the way, the specific name of this sacrament, the name which distinguishes it from the others, is "Penance," not reconciliation. The Eucharist is the sacrament *of* reconciliation; penance is a sacrament *for* reconciliation. The Eucharist celebrates the reconciliation brought about by penance.]

The Acts of the Penitent

The essential means for participation in the sacrament of penance are called "the acts of the penitent." They are contrition, confession, and satisfaction. The Introduction to the Rite of Penance in the ritual states that "the most important act of the penitent is contrition, which is a heartfelt sorrow and aversion for the sin committed along with the intention of sinning no more."[2] Contrition says, "I wish I had not done that. If I had another chance, I would really try not to be guilty of that sin." True contrition leads to an open, honest expression of our sins.

---

[1] *Constitution on the Sacred Liturgy*, no. 14.
[2] Introduction to the Rite of Penance, 6a. The definition in this Introduction is taken from the Council of Trent, Session XIV.

That is the second act, confession. The third is satisfaction, which we popularly have termed "the penance." The Introduction says that "conversion is completed by acts of penance or satisfaction for the sins committed, by amendment of conduct, and by the reparation of injury." An honest confession includes contrition and leads to satisfaction.

You may have heard someone say that because of contrition your sins are usually forgiven long before you actually go to confession. That seems to imply that the sacrament is little more than a celebration of forgiveness, but such is not the case. The sacrament does not begin when the penitent approaches a priest. The sacrament begins with the initial stirring of contrition, which is the first act of the penitent and which may develop over some period of time. The grace of the sacrament is at work in a person who is moving toward contrition.

Here is an example of how grace can work. One morning as a couple are sitting down to breakfast, their twenty-two-year-old daughter, Karen, comes in the kitchen door. She is glowing. She holds out her left hand, palm down, and says, "Mom and Dad, look at that ring! Philip proposed to me last night." After hugs of congratulations, Karen leaves to go to her job. Her parents, Bob and Joan, look at each other for a few moments, and then Joan says what both have been thinking, "You know, Bob, we are going to have to receive communion at that wedding and we must go to confession before that." Bob merely nods and goes back to his newspaper. The problem they both recognized was that since Karen had moved out of the house three years earlier, Bob and Joan had not been to Mass except once at Christmas.

In the months that followed the subject of the wedding and what it would involve for them occasionally came up in their conversation. Then early one Saturday evening just a week before the wedding, Bob came home and said to Joan, "You will never guess what I did. After my golf game, I drove over to Miraculous Medal Church where we were married and I went to confession." Joan could not hide her smile. She said, "And you will never guess what I did. After you left for your golf game, I was downtown and I passed St. Vincent's Church on Adams Boulevard. I decided to go in. A priest was just finishing Mass, and I asked him to hear my confession, which he did."

Bob and Joan began to form the sacrament of penance from the moment that Karen told them about the wedding. They were a channel of grace to each other in their conversation, and just passing St. Vincent's Church was for Joan what theologians call an external grace. Actually even the announcement about the wedding was an external grace.[3] When each finally went to confession, the sacrament had been taking shape for months and forming within them the first act of the penitent, which is contrition. Their contrition led them to the second act of the penitent, which is confession.

The Introduction to the Rite of Penance in the ritual states: "Confession of sins requires that penitents be willing to open their hearts to the minister of God."[4] Changing the rule which required a screen between priest and penitent has helped people to fulfill this directive. (The original purpose of the screen was not to insure anonymity but to satisfy sexual propriety: only women were obliged to confess behind a screen.) The experi-

---

[3] Actual grace, divine help, is internal but God makes use of external factors as a channel for his internal grace. These external factors are sometimes termed external graces.

[4] Introduction to the Rite of Penance, 6b.

ence was very impersonal. Like other priests, at times I have presumed that the voice I was hearing was that of a woman, only to realize during the confession that it was that of a young boy. That and similar situations can be very awkward.

Removing the screen does not guarantee a heartfelt confession. First must come a proper examination of conscience. I have found that a fruitful examination of conscience follows the well founded formula: "What did I do? Why did I do it? What do I intend to do about it?" The answer to the first question should be descriptive and not merely a statement. St. Augustine said that the motive makes the deed. That is why the second question is important: "Why did I do it?" The answer to the third question indicates the purpose of amendment.

Let's say that Bob in preparation for his daughter's wedding goes to confession (all this is entirely imaginary). He says to the priest, "I missed Mass for about three years. I didn't say daily prayers. At times I got upset with my wife." That manner of confessing is not what is meant by "opening your heart" to the priest. In contrast to this confession, let's say that Bob in examining his conscience follows the formula, "What did I do? Why did I do it? What do I intend to do about it?" His confession then is like this (purely imaginary, of course): "Father, I haven't been going to Mass for the past three years. My wife and I stopped going when our daughter got her own apartment. We had only one child whom we loved very much. We wanted the best for her. I was never a very serious Catholic, but I thought it was important to give our child a religion, the Catholic religion in particular. So over the years I went to church every Sunday without thinking about it very much. I did it just for the sake of our daughter. I feel like I have been a little bit of a hypocrite, but now our little girl is getting married and I want to do the right thing. In thinking about her wedding I realize how good God was to us during all those years when she was growing up and I really ought to be a better Catholic out of gratitude to God. My wife and I talked about this and we have made up our minds that we are going to start going to Mass again every Sunday."

That is a fruitful confession. When Bob left the priest, he felt good because the sacrament helped to heal him through his own grace-aided efforts. Even in confession "the aim to be considered before all else is full, active participation." Bob did not mention his daily prayers or his impatience with his wife. That can come in another confession. He was right to concentrate on one serious matter.

Next is satisfaction. This third act of the penitent should be suited to the person and to the sin. It should be an antidote to sin, "a remedy for sin and a help to renewal of life."[5] (That is why there should never be a "general penance" for everyone when the second rite is celebrated.) In Bob's case, the priest might pick up on the fact that he said, "I really ought to be a better Catholic out of gratitude to God." That could suggest that for his "penance" Bob should spend some time in church counting his blessings, recalling all the good things God has done for him, and then resolving that he will make Sunday Mass a true Eucharist, a thanksgiving to God. After the priest proposes the act of penance and Bob accepts it, the priest asks him to express his sorrow (the act of contrition). When Bob leaves the church, the grace of the sacrament can still be working in him. Just as contrition begins before a person goes to the priest, so

---

[5] Introduction to the Rite of Penance, 6c.

satisfaction can continue after he leaves the priest. Bob may even spend the evening talking to his wife about how grateful he realizes he should be and how much better he feels about things.

A story is that a man went to confession and began by saying "My last confession was yesterday." When the priest asked him why he had returned so soon, he replied "Because my penance was to say the rosary every day until my next confession." That penance was not what the Church has in mind for satisfaction which is suited to the penitent and to his sin.

The Prayer of Absolution

In the sacrament of penance, priest and penitent together form the sacrament just as priest and people together celebrate the Mass. As we have seen the penitent has three actions, sometimes called the "matter" of the sacrament. The priest's action, sometimes called the form of the sacrament, is absolution. The essential words of absolution in the formula in use just before the Second Vatican Council were succinct. Translated from Latin they were "May our Lord Jesus Christ absolve you, and by his authority I absolve you from your sins in the name of the Father, and of the Son, and of the Holy Spirit." The penitent made his act of contrition while the priest recited the Latin formula.

The *Constitution on the Sacred Liturgy* made only this simple statement: "The rite and formulas for the sacrament of penance are to be revised so that they give more luminous expression to both the nature and the effect of the sacrament."[6]

---

[6] *Constitution on the Sacred Liturgy*, no. 72.

The revised formula for absolution expresses the action of the Trinity, the ministry of the Church, the fruit of the sacrament, and the meaning of forgiveness. That formula is: "God the Father of mercies through the death and resurrection of his Son has reconciled the world to himself and sent the Holy Spirit among us for the forgiveness of sins; through the ministry of the Church may God give you pardon and peace, and I absolve you from your sins in the name of the Father and of the Son and of the Holy Spirit."

The formula begins: "God...." That is the right place to start since sin offends God and only God and forgive it. Our God, however, is not a God of wrath. Our God is the Father of mercies. Note that the word is in the plural, "mercies." The Latin for "mercies" is a big, long word, *misericordiarum*. God's mercies are not only big, they are great. His mercies last not only a long time, but forever. In the Latin of the First Eucharistic Prayer we tell God that we hope in the multitude of his mercies, "*de multitudine miserationum tuarum*" (rather weakly translated as "we hope in your mercy and love"). We experience God's mercies not as an intangible virtue, which might be termed "mercy" in the singular, but as his loving actions toward us in the plural, especially as they are seen in the gospel narratives of his Son. We should readily think of the woman caught in adultery whom Jesus refused to condemn, the paralytic to whom he said, "Your sins are forgiven," the leper whom he touched and healed. Almost every Sunday gospel proclaims to us the multitude of God the Father's mercies in the actions of his Son.

The word "mercies" does not denote pity. [See Chapter 11 of Book 2 on the "Lord, have mercy."] God does not pity us as if we were wretched creatures. God acts in accord with his covenant of love which began in the Old Testament era and which reached a new and deeper commitment in the death of Jesus. Psalm 117 celebrates God's covenant of mercies in these words: "Strong is his love for us; he is faithful for ever." God renews and strengthens his covenant in us through the cross of Jesus, as we hear proclaimed during the eucharistic prayer: "This is the cup of my blood, the blood of the new and everlasting covenant." In many ways, but especially in the sacrament of penance, God showers us with his mercies.

The prayer of absolution continues: "God the Father of mercies through the death and resurrection of his Son...." The paschal mystery of the death and resurrection of Jesus is the central mystery of the incarnation. Everything flows from the paschal mystery. In the sacrament of penance we share in the death of Jesus, a dying to sin. Jesus by dying destroyed our death, the eternal death of sin. We share in the resurrection, a renewal of life. Jesus by rising has restored our life, the life of God's grace.

The Father of mercies through the death and resurrection of his Son "has reconciled the world to himself." That sounds rather cosmic, and it is. St. Paul writes these mysterious words: "Indeed the whole created world eagerly awaits the revelation of the children of God.... The world itself will be freed from its slavery to corruption and share in the glorious freedom of the children of God. Yes, we know that all creation groans and is in agony even until now."[7] That agony is being overcome through the paschal mystery by which God the Father reconciles the world to himself.

The words of absolution say further that God the Father "has sent the Holy Spirit among us for the forgiveness of sins." Now that is more personal, and more understandable. The Holy

---

[7] Romans 8:19-22.

Spirit is the bond of love uniting God the Father and God the Son in an eternal embrace of love. Sin separates. Forgiveness reunites. That is the work of the Holy Spirit. In the second Epiclesis of the eucharistic prayer we express the power of the Holy Spirit to bring about unity: "May all of us who share in the body and blood of Christ be brought together in unity by the Holy Spirit."

Next the priest says, "Through the ministry of the Church...." In the sacrament of penance it is not that both God and the Church grant forgiveness, but that God grants forgiveness through the Church. God's way has been to take the human way, to act toward us through the visible and audible elements of the sacraments of the Church. The prayer of the priest is that "through the ministry of the Church may God grant you pardon and peace." Pardon leads to peace, peace of mind and peace of heart. What a great blessing that is, to be at peace. After confession we should feel good, relieved of a burden, light hearted, and at peace.

Then come the great climactic words spoken in the first person singular, the "Great I," which is not the person of the priest but the person of Christ speaking through the priest: "I absolve you from your sins." What a great word "absolve" is. It is an unusual word, one we do not use very often, and God's forgiveness is unusual. God's forgiveness is an absolution. The word has a ring of finality about it. It means that God is the king who, when the servant pleaded for a delay in payment, gave more than he was asked and wiped out the debt completely. God cancels the guilt of sin through his Son.[8] St. Paul wrote to the Colossians: "God pardoned all our sins. He canceled the

---

[8] Matthew 18:21-35.

bond that stood against us with all its claims, snatching it up and nailing it to the cross."[9] Jesus "in his own body brought our sins to the cross so that all of us, dead to sin, could live in accord with God's will."[10] What a peace-granting reality absolution is!

The Second Vatican Council directed that "the rite and formulas for the sacrament of penance are to be revised so that they give more luminous expression to both the nature and the effect of the sacrament."[11] The words of absolution have complied with that directive.

The Three Rites of Penance

The Vatican Council also directed that "It is to be stressed that whenever rites, according to their specific nature, make provision for communal celebration involving the presence and active participation of the faithful, this way of celebrating them is to be preferred, as far as possible, to a celebration that is individual and quasi-private."[12] When those words were written in 1963 the vast majority of Catholics had experienced the sacrament of penance in a very private and individualistic manner behind a screen. (Some few had participated in general absolution in war-time situations.) The concilium after the Council had to set about to provide a new way of celebrating penance. After much discussion and debate the decision was made to provide three rites or forms of the one sacrament of penance.

---

[9] Colossians 2:14.
[10] 1 Peter 2:24.
[11] *Constitution on the Sacred Liturgy*, no. 72.
[12] *Ibid.*, no. 27.

The First Rite

The first form is officially designated as "The Rite for the Reconciliation of Individual Penitents." The priest is instructed to welcome the penitent warmly and to greet him or her with kindness. The penitent makes the sign of the cross, which the priest may make also. In a few words the priest invites the penitent to trust in God. There is a brief selection from the word of God. The priest may read a passage or even recite one from memory. Some penitents may wish to choose and read their own selection. (Unfortunately the rite describes the reading of the word of God as optional.) The penitent confesses his sins. The priest may offer some words of counsel. He proposes an act of penance which the penitent accepts to amend his life. The penitent expresses his sorrow (the act of contrition) and the priest proclaims absolution. The rite concludes with an expression of praise and thanks which may be as simple as the priest's saying, "Let us give thanks to the Lord our God," to which the penitent responds, "His mercy endures forever." The priest then "dismisses" the penitent by saying something like, "Your sins are forgiven. Go in peace."

The distinctive value of this first rite is the grace of spiritual healing which comes from the confession of sins. We all know that it is good to get something off your chest. That human experiences takes on a transcendent meaning in the sacrament of penance. After confession the penitent should feel good, light hearted, relieved of a burden.

The Second Rite

The second form of the sacrament is officially designated as "The Rite for the Reconciliation of Many Penitents with Individual Confession and Absolution."[13] In popular parlance, it is known simply, although inaccurately, as "A Penance Service." This second rite is a commendable attempt to make the sacrament look more like liturgy by providing a communal form of celebration in accord with the wishes of the *Constitution on the Sacred Liturgy*, as noted above. The first part of the rite is a Liturgy of the Word and resembles that part of the Mass. Following the homily there is a time for examination of conscience. Then the assembly makes a general confession of sins. It is beneficial to use the familiar "I confess," which is also used at Mass, for the general confession of sins. It is humble and honest, and reflects our Catholic doctrine of the Mystical Body of Christ and the Communion of Saints. "I confess to almighty God and to you, my brothers and sisters." That is correct. Sin in the first place offends God but every sin, even the most secret, has social effects as well. We are all hurt in some way by sin. "…that I have sinned through my own fault." What honesty and humility! No excuses! I do not have to be afraid to admit that I have sinned through my own fault since I am confident I will receive God's forgiveness through the ministry of the Church. "…in my thoughts and in my words, in what I have done, and in what I have failed to do." That is admirably inclusive. "And I ask blessed Mary, ever virgin, all the angels and saints, and you, my brothers and sisters, to pray for me to the Lord our God." That is the Communion of Saints in action.

---

[13] Some English translations have "for several penitents," but the Latin *pluribus* is better rendered as "many."

Following the general confession of sinfulness there is a litany of praise which concludes with the Lord's Prayer (the latter is always to be included). So far so good on the communal aspects of the rite but at the crucial moment there is a deviation: the rite calls for individual confession and absolution as in the first rite. That returns the sacrament to a quasi-private experience. Everyone is invited to remain until the end for the Proclamation of Praise for God's Mercy and the Concluding Prayer of Thanksgiving. It is a mistake to skip the ceremony after individual confessions. That ceremony is integral to the rite. Even though some people may really find it necessary to leave after their personal confession, everyone should be encouraged to remain until the end, in order both to spend time in prayer for all those who are confessing their sins, and to participate in the concluding expression of thanksgiving.

An excellent prayer to offer in union with those who are confessing their sins is Psalm 32:

> Happy the one whose offense is forgiven,
> whose sin is remitted.
> O happy the one to whom the Lord
> imputes no guilt.
>
> "I kept my sin secret and my frame was wasted.
> I groaned all day long
> for night and day your hand
> was heavy upon me.
> Indeed, my strength was dried up
> as by the summer's heat.
> But now I have acknowledged my sins;
> my guilt I did not hide.
> I said: 'I will confess

my offense to the Lord.'
And you, Lord, have forgiven
the guilt of my sin.
So let every good person pray to you
in time of need."[14]

An excellent prayer of thanksgiving is the *Magnificat* of
Mary. Also very suitable is Psalm 103:

My soul, give thanks to the Lord,
all my being, bless his holy name.
My soul, give thanks to the Lord
and never forget all his blessings.
It is he who forgives all your guilt,
who heals every one of your ills,
who redeems your life from the grave,
who crowns you with love and compassion,
who fills your life with good things.
The Lord is compassion and love,
slow to anger and rich in mercy.
He does not treat us according to our sins
nor repay us according to our faults.
For as the heavens are high above the earth
so strong is his love for those who fear him.
As far as the east is from the west
so far does he remove our sins.
As a father has compassion on his sons,
the Lord has compassion on those who fear him.[15]

---

[14] This psalm is found at Evening Prayer on Thursday of Week I. I have included
only excerpts from the psalm.

[15] These are excerpts from the psalm which can be found in its entirety at the Office
of Readings for Wednesday of Week IV.

This second rite is a compromise. It expresses some of the communal aspects which are found to the full in the third rite while preserving the benefits to be derived from individual confession of sins in the first rite. Many parishes, perhaps the majority in the United States, celebrate the Second Rite of Penance twice a year, during Advent and Lent. To make this rite effective, priests must join together from other parishes and assignments to be confessors. Some deaneries have the practice of rotating a monthly penance service among participating parishes, a very commendable idea.

The Third Rite

The third form of the sacrament is termed "The Rite for Reconciliation of Many Penitents with General Confession and Absolution." It looks very much like the Second Rite except that there is no individual confession of sins and no individual absolution. Usually it is referred to simply as "General Absolution," but it is far from being usual. The current legislation is very restrictive. The *Code of Canon Law* states: "Absolution cannot be imparted in a general manner to a number of penitents at once without previous individual confession unless:

(1) the danger of death is imminent and there is not time for the priest or priests to hear the confessions of the individual penitents;

(2) a serious necessity exists, that is, when in the light of the number of penitents a supply of confessors is not readily available rightly to hear the confessions of individuals within a suitable time so that the penitents are forced to be deprived of sacramental grace or Holy Communion for a long time through

no fault of their own; it is not considered a sufficient necessity if confessors cannot be readily available only because of the great number of penitents as can occur on the occasion of some great feast or pilgrimage."[16] The law also states that it is for the diocesan bishop to judge whether conditions allow for general absolution. Even when general absolution is granted, "a person who is conscious of grave sin must intend to confess individually the serious sins which at present cannot be confessed."[17]

This law is very intent upon preserving the benefits of individual confession as well as maintaining the requirement that all grave sins must be submitted to the sacrament, but it seems too restrictive. First it does not honor the old maxim, *sacramenta propter homines*, sacraments are for people. The Church should be generous in sharing the sacraments. People deserve to find the sacrament of penance readily available to them. Although only mortal sins must be confessed and other sins may be forgiven by an act of contrition or a devout sharing in the Eucharist, the normal means of forgiveness for Catholics should be through the sacrament of penance. The sacraments — all of them — are the Catholic way. A deep appreciation of the value of this sacrament, it seems to me, urges that it be more readily available through the third rite. Secondly, this restrictive law does not aid in developing the awareness that penance is a liturgy which offers praise and thanksgiving to the God of forgiveness. God's forgiveness is such an excellent quality that Catholics should be encouraged to come together in large numbers to celebrate that forgiveness by participating in the sacrament of penance. Thirdly, the current law does not foster the com-

---

[16] Canon 961.
[17] Canon 962.

munal aspect of the sacrament. Finally I cannot pass over the fact that general absolution requires the service of only one priest — not an insignificant consideration in a time of the shortage of priests.

Whatever the manner of celebrating, it is vital to note that the sacrament of penance is liturgical. It worships the God of forgiveness, enhances the unity of the Church, and leads to the celebration of the Eucharist.

ANOINTING OF THE SICK

"Is there anyone sick among you? He should ask for the presbyters of the Church." (James 5:14)

It is the year 1950. A dark colored Ford automobile pulls up to the curb just outside the house at 2612 Palmyra Street. A priest emerges from the automobile. All of his clothing is black except for his white roman collar and a thin purple stole around his neck. In his hand he carries a small satchel. Neighbors peering out of their window whisper, "It looks like old Mrs. Flanagan is about to meet her Maker." They know that the priest has come for the last rites. In his satchel he has the holy oil for extreme unction, the last anointing.

This scene could not have taken place before the twelfth century, not only because automobiles had obviously not yet been invented, but because the sacrament was originally understood to be for the spiritual and physical benefit of a person who was seriously ill but who was not necessarily about to die. The sacrament of dying was Holy Communion as viaticum. It still is today.

History is not clear on the reason for the transition of anointing from being a sacrament for the sick to a sacrament for the dying. It may have been that an effort to relate the sacraments to moments in life placed anointing, rather than Holy Communion as viaticum, at the end of our journey.[18] In any event, Peter Lombard (who died in 1160) seems to have been the first to use the term "extreme unction," the last anointing.

The Second Vatican Council in its *Constitution on the Sacred Liturgy* restored the traditional understanding of this sacrament. It taught that "extreme unction" is more fittingly called "The Anointing of the Sick." The Council also indicated that "this sacrament is not only for those who are at the point of death; hence, as soon as any one of the faithful begins to be in danger of death from sickness or old age, the appropriate time for this sacrament has certainly already arrived."[19] The new Rite of Anointing in the General Introduction adds: "A prudent or reasonably sure judgment about the danger of death, made by the pastor or the priest, is sufficient; in such a case, there is no reason for scruples." Other points made by the General Introduction are: "A sick person may be anointed before surgery whenever a serious illness is the reason for surgery. Elderly people may be anointed if they have become notably weakened even though no serious illness is present. Sick children may be anointed if they have sufficient use of reason to be strengthened by this sacrament."

---

[18] In the same thinking confirmation began to be seen as the sacrament of maturity rather than as part of Christian initiation. The attempt to establish a parallel between the sacraments and important moments in life resulted in this type of schema: We are born by baptism, nourished by the Eucharist, grow up in confirmation, confess our sins in penance, get married or are ordained, and get ready for death by extreme unction.

[19] *Constitution on the Sacred Liturgy*, no. 73.

People make a grave mistake who fail to call a priest for loved ones who are seriously ill with the excuse that they do not want to frighten them. An important pastoral principle from the General Instruction must be emphasized: "The faithful should be educated to ask for the sacrament as soon as the right time comes, to receive it with full faith and devotion. They should not follow the wrongful practice of delaying the reception of this sacrament." The General Introduction follows the principle, *sacramenta propter homines*.

This sacrament flows from the teaching of St. James in his epistle: "Is anyone among you sick? He should summon the presbyters of the church, and they should pray over him and anoint him with oil in the name of the Lord, and the prayer of faith will save the sick person, and the Lord will raise him up. If he has committed any sins, he will be forgiven."[20] In fulfillment of the words of St. James, the priest anoints the sick person on the forehead and on the hands while saying, "Through this holy anointing may the Lord in his love and mercy help you with the grace of the Holy Spirit. May the Lord who frees you from sin save you and raise you up." The last verb can be understood as a prayer that the sick person will be raised up from a sick bed and as a prayer that the sick person will be raised up on the last day.[21]

The classic scriptural text associated with the anointing of the sick is that from James, but a remarkable illustration of the sacrament is found in Mark's gospel: "Jesus entered the house of Simon and Andrew with James and John. Simon's mother-

---

[20] James 5:14-15.
[21] "Raise up" may be stretching the meaning of the Latin, *"allevet,"* but the translation is theologically sound.

in-law lay ill with a fever, and the first thing they did was to tell him about her. He went over to her and grasped her hand and helped her up, and the fever left her. She immediately began to wait on them."[22] Consider the situation. The woman was sick, apparently confined to bed because of her fever. She was seriously ill. The brothers, Peter and Andrew, told Jesus about her. They represent those who are so concerned about persons who are ill that they call in the priest. Jesus in the sacrament acts through his priest and in effect takes the sick persons by the hand and raises them up. If it be God's will, those who are ill are restored to health so that, like Peter's mother-in-law, they may return to the service of others.

It is commendable to celebrate the anointing of the sick in a communal celebration, especially during Mass, but only those who are seriously ill are to be anointed. It is not correct to follow an opinion that we are all sick in some way and so we all may come forward to be anointed.

All liturgical sacraments have three effects and center on the Eucharist. Since this sacrament is liturgical, it offers praise and thanks to the God of healing. That paramount truth must be emphasized since it seems far from the thinking of many people. Secondly the sacrament helps to overcome illness, and gives strength for the person to return to an active life in the Church, the family, and the community. When people are seriously ill, they have to turn their attention to themselves. Good people regret that they must abandon their duties and leave to others the work they would ordinarily do themselves. This sacrament helps to restore those who are ill to their rightful place

---

[22] Mark 1:29-30. St. Luke tells the same story in 4:38-39.

of service to others (as was Peter's mother-in-law). God's ultimate act of healing we will experience in the resurrection, which is the promise offered to us in the Eucharist.

FUNERALS

"Jesus began to weep." (John 11:35)

A Catholic funeral is the worst of times, and it is the best of times. It is the worst of times because it is like Jesus standing before the tomb of his beloved friend, Lazarus, and weeping. It is the best of times because it is like hearing the voice of Jesus before the tomb saying, "Come forth."

The two aspects of death are acknowledged in the Preface for the Dead: "The sadness of death gives way to the bright promise of immortality." Our time of grief is important and necessary but our sadness is gradually to lessen, and even to fade away, since "in him who rose from the dead our hope of resurrection has dawned." We believe "that life is changed, not ended, and when the body of our earthly dwelling lies in death we gain an everlasting dwelling place in heaven."[23] A woman asked a priest to speak to her wealthy but very elderly husband. She said that she could not convince him that when he had to go, he could not take his wealth with him. After the priest spoke with her husband, she asked him how he had done. The priest replied, "I couldn't even convince him that he had to go." But go in death we all must, and yet when we do so with firm faith in

---

[23] Preface 77, Christian Death I.

the promises of Christ we can depart with all the riches of the virtue of hope.

There is no sacrament of Christian burial. The reason is that death is the final step into the paschal mystery of the death and resurrection of Jesus, the mystery of which the Eucharist is the sacrament. Baptism was our first sharing in the paschal mystery. That is why the casket should be draped in white, recalling the white robe of baptism.[24] Baptism is celebrated in every Eucharist and completed in death. We all must make the passage with Christ through the dark, awesome doors of death in order to emerge into everlasting life. By dying he destroyed our death, and by rising he restored our life. Our death is conjoined to his and our dying too is a triumph over the finality of death. The act of dying contains the pledge of rising to everlasting life. These great truths are celebrated in every Eucharist but in a special way during a funeral.

The term, "Mass of the Resurrection," should not be applied to funerals, as the Bishops' Committee on the Liturgy has pointed out. The celebration of Easter is unique; it alone deserves the title, "Mass of the Resurrection." The proper term at a funeral is "Mass of Christian Burial." The Christian passage reflects the sacred triduum. The day of our death is our personal Good Friday. Our time in the grave, however long it may be, is our personal Holy Saturday. Our resurrection from the dead will be our personal Easter Sunday.

---

[24] Although violet, even black, vestments may still be used at a funeral, white is by far the preferred color.

Chapter 5

The Concept of the Liturgical Year

"These are the festivals of the Lord, my feast days, which you shall celebrate with a sacred assembly." (Leviticus 23:2)

TIME IS AN ELUSIVE REALITY. We all experience it but we fail to comprehend its full significance. A year, which is one way in which we measure time, is 365 days, 5 hours, 48 minutes, and 46 seconds. Having looked that up, I do not feel that I am any closer to understanding time. Aristotle said that time is the "measure of motion or change according to before and after." If that means something, I suppose you could apply his definition to a lot of reality, including a life span, but I find Aristotle's notion not very helpful. Albert Einstein's general theory of relativity leaves me baffled, especially the principle that "space and time are interdependent and form a four-dimensional continuum." What was that again?

I am confident both philosophically and theologically that God is beyond time, that God transcends time, that God is eternal. With God all is present, nothing is past, nothing is future. Of course, I comprehend the eternity of God even less than I do the general theory of relativity, but we will see later that the eternity of God does have an important bearing on the topic of this chapter.

Turning to something simpler, I recognize that the idea most contemporary people, especially historians, have of time is that it is a series of unrepeatable events, one following upon another. Time is like a straight line with a beginning, a middle, and an end. Some historians do not like to hear us say that history repeats itself since in their view it cannot do so, at least not in a literal sense. Historical events are confined to the past and cannot be duplicated. There is no way to clone time.

The ancients had a different understanding of time. They lived close to the land and were dependent upon their observations of nature for their livelihood. They saw time as a cycle, as a series of events which regularly repeat themselves. Spring is a period of beginning, a bright fresh season of hope and promise, the moment of planting. Summer is for the growth and maturation of crops under the warm, nourishing rays of the sun upon which the ancients depended as upon a god. Fall means the harvest, the opportunity to reap the fruits of labor. Fall, however, turns into winter, with its cold, dark, seemingly endless nights and altogether brief days as the light fades and the sun appears almost to die. But there is no reason to lose hope since inevitably winter turns into spring and the cycle is repeated.[1]

The liturgy rather favors the idea of the ancients since the liturgy itself is ancient. In fact, we all recognize that we celebrate the same events in a yearly cycle. Vatican II's *Constitution on the Sacred Liturgy* states that very fact for us: "Within the cycle

---

[1]   Of course matters are just the opposite in the southern hemisphere from what they are in the northern, which makes something of a problem for a universal Church when it comes to the liturgical symbolism of time.

of the year, the Church unfolds the whole mystery of Christ, not only from his Incarnation and birth until his Ascension, but also as reflected in the day of Pentecost and the expectation of a blessed, hope-for return of the Lord."[2]

This teaching follows upon that of Pope Pius XII who was a little more complete in his encyclical, *Mediator Dei*, in 1947: "In the sacred liturgy the whole Christ is proposed to us in all the circumstances of his life, as the Word of the Eternal Father, as born of the Virgin Mother of God, as he who teaches us truth, heals the sick, consoles the afflicted, who endures suffering and who dies; finally, as he who rose triumphantly from the dead and who, reigning in the glory of heaven, sends us the Holy Spirit who abides in his Church forever."[3] The *Constitution on the Sacred Liturgy* goes on to insist that "Recalling the mysteries of redemption, the Church opens to the faithful the riches of her Lord's powers and merits, so that these are in some way made present at all times and the faithful are enabled to lay hold of them and become filled with saving grace."[4] And this teaching of the Council flows from that of Pope Pius XII in *Mediator Dei*: "The Liturgical Year is not a cold and lifeless representation of the events of the past, or a simple and bare record of a former age. It is rather Christ himself who is ever living in his Church.... These mysteries are ever present and active among us."[5]

---

[2] *Constitution on the Sacred Liturgy*, no. 102.
[3] *Mediator Dei*, no. 163.
[4] *Constitution on the Sacred Liturgy*, no. 102.
[5] *Mediator Dei*, no. 165.

Extraordinary Liturgical Doctrine

The marvel of the liturgical year makes me think back to the big, academy award-winning movie *Titanic*. One of the untold stories of the fateful voyage is that on board the ship was a magician who on the night of the disaster performed a magic show in the ship's auditorium. He first did a card trick, but a little boy in the front row stood up and explained to the audience how it was done. And so for every act of magic the little boy had an explanation. Then the magician pulled a rabbit from a hat and quickly made hat and rabbit disappear. Just as the little boy was explaining that feat, the *Titanic* hit the iceberg. In all of the confusion of trying to get to the deck, the magician was swept overboard. As the ship disappeared under the water, he came to, clinging instinctively to a huge beam of wood. He opened his eyes to see the little boy, sitting with arms folded, at the end of the beam. The little boy said, "O.K., I give up. What did you do with the ship?"

There is no magic about the liturgical year, only a profound mystery which is reflected in the truth that the Church embraces an extraordinary doctrine about the liturgical year. We do not merely observe anniversaries of past events, as we do Washington's birthday or the signing of the *Declaration of Independence*. Washington is dead and is buried; so is that historical event of his birth into this world. The signing of the *Declaration of Independence* was a crucial moment in the life of our country but it is consigned to the past and cannot be repeated. It is history. Not so the life of Jesus Christ. Jesus is not dead. He is alive and active in the sacred liturgy and brings with him all the events of his wonderful life. Remember that Pius XII declared that Christ is ever living in his Church and his mysteries are ever present and active among us.

Pope Leo the Great, who was pope from 440 to 461, said in a Christmas homily: "Although the state of infancy, which the Son of God did not disdain to assume, developed with the passage of time into the maturity of manhood, and although after the triumph of the passion and the resurrection all his lowly acts undertaken on our behalf belong to the past, nevertheless today's feast of Christmas renews for us the sacred beginning of Jesus' life, his birth from the Virgin Mary."[6]

St. Francis of Assisi is credited with creating the first Christmas crib. He told his friend, John da Vellita, "I would make a memorial of that Christ who was born in Bethlehem and in some sort behold with bodily eyes the hardships of his infant state, lying on hay in a manger with the ox and the ass standing by." In 1223 he set up a crib at his hermitage in Grecchio, Italy and from that day the practice has spread throughout the whole world.[7] The crib is now an important liturgical symbol. We have surrounded birthdays with customs such as a decorating a cake with candles and the singing of "Happy birthday to you," but in no instance do we set up a painting or picture or any depiction of the day of birth. The reason is that we are celebrating the *anniversary* of one's birth. The Christmas crib reminds us that we are not celebrating the anniversary of Jesus' birth but the very birth itself. In the liturgy by the almighty power of God, Christmas is the actualization of the birth of Jesus for us.

Our doctrine of the liturgical year is a continuation of the Old Testament understanding of liturgical celebrations. This

---

[6] See the Office of Readings for Dec. 31.
[7] *Butler's Lives of the Saints, Concise Edition,* page 319.

understanding is particularly exemplified in the deuteronomic literature within which salvific events of the past are told as occurring to the people of the present — because they were. The Book of Deuteronomy consists mainly of sermons on the Book of Exodus which were composed centuries after the events which it relates. The preacher speaks in the person of Moses. His purpose is to proclaim again the ancient tradition in a time of great crisis for Israel. His message is not "Thus said the Lord God" in the past tense, but "Thus says the Lord God" in the present tense.

Consider the great profession of faith in Deuteronomy 26:5-6 which was proclaimed within a liturgical celebration. Note the subtle change from the third person to the first: "A wandering Aramean was my father who went down to Egypt with a small household and lived there as an alien. But there he became a nation great, strong and numerous. When the Egyptians maltreated and oppressed us (this is the sudden change to the first person, to the people living long after the event), imposing hard labor on us, we cried to the Lord, the God of our fathers, and he heard our cry and saw our affliction, our toil and our oppression. He brought us out of Egypt with his strong hand and outstretched arm, with terrifying power, with signs and wonders; and bringing us into this country, he gave us this land flowing with milk and honey."

Psalm 126 is another example. It is the song of the exiles who returned from the Babylonian captivity: "When the Lord delivered Zion from bondage, it seemed like a dream." Those who prayed this psalm generations after the event included themselves: "Then *our* mouth filled with laughter, on *our* lips there were songs." They thought back to the reaction of pagan neighbors upon the return of the exiles: "The heathen themselves said: 'What marvels the Lord worked for them,'" but those praying the psalm insisted, "What marvels the Lord worked for *us!*"

Our theology of the liturgical year follows the Old Testament theology of liturgy.

I am always amazed when I realize that many people satisfy themselves with merely reading the Bible when through the liturgy of the Church they could actually enter into the events of the Bible.

To understand the reality of the liturgical year it is helpful to refer to our theology of transubstantiation. In the Eucharist the substance of bread and wine are changed into the body and the blood of the Lord, while the accidents are not affected. In the liturgical year the substance of the mysteries of Christ become present without the accidents. This means, for example, that the grace-filled moment of the birth of Jesus is with us at Christmas but not the cold of Bethlehem, and that his preaching reaches our ears but without our seeing the terrain upon which he stood, and that we are confirmed in faith by means of the transfiguration without seeing the splendor of his countenance as did Peter, James, and John. The liturgical year is real, not imaginary, and yet it is a mystery. A "Rahnerism" helps us: "A mystery is not a truth about which we can know nothing. It is a truth about which we cannot know everything." We cannot comprehend the mystery of the liturgical year but what we do understand about it leads us to full, active participation in liturgical celebrations.

The Liturgical "Now"

Have we neglected this beautiful doctrine of the liturgical year? Let's think about its meaning further. Some liturgical scholars refer to the reality of liturgical celebration as the liturgical "now." There is a "here and now" about liturgical celebrations because of "anamnesis," which is liturgical memorial. This is where the eternity of God finds application. God the Father holds all the events of the life of his Son in his eternal memory, where all events are neither past nor future but only present. Through the power of the liturgy God the Father lifts us up into his eternal memory. There we not only remember but actually enter into the events of the life of God's beloved Son. All liturgical celebrations are anamnesis, but in particular there is a sacrament of anamnesis for the paschal mystery, the death and resurrection of Jesus, and that is the holy Eucharist. The holy Eucharist is the *living* memorial of his death and resurrection. Our celebration of the Eucharist fulfills Jesus' commandment: "Do this in memory of me." Jesus has given us a sacrament which is the anamnesis of the paschal mystery, his death and resurrection, because all the events of his life which we celebrate in the liturgy are fulfilled, caught up, gathered together in his death and resurrection. From the moment that Jesus was conceived in Mary's womb, he was destined to follow and complete the Father's plan according to which he would destroy death by dying and restore life by rising. When he was born into our world, he was already pointed toward Jerusalem where he would fulfill the paschal mystery. A mere forty days after his birth he was offered to God in the temple in anticipation of his offering of himself on the cross. At twelve he was found (where else?)

in his Father's house, the temple of Jerusalem which he would replace with his own body. In his public ministry he was on a relentless journey up to the Holy City where he would accomplish the purpose of his birth so that by his cross and resurrection he would set us free. His paschal mystery is his declaration of our independence from sin and death and our birth as the Church, the people of God.

The expression is always to go "up" to Jerusalem, regardless of the direction from which one comes, since the city is on a mountain. When people set out to climb a mountain, they have to make many preparations. They need proper equipment, supplies, a map of the face of the mountain, and a plan. The climb is tortuous as they sometimes slip and skin knees and elbows, or become entangled in shrubs, and in a moment of alarm come close to falling to the rocks beneath them. Often when asked why they go to all the trouble of scaling a mountain, the climbers reply, "Because it is there." More than that, however, they feel a deep sense of accomplishment when they have reached the top. The moment of victory makes it all worthwhile. In a sense all the efforts to get to the top are present with them when they reach the summit.

All of this is said in reference to Jesus. Everything about him found its purpose on the mountain on which Jerusalem was located. All the preparations during the period of the Old Testament, including God's covenant, the teachings of the prophets and the destiny of the people led to his coming into our world. That was the Father's plan. He gave his Son a map to follow but the way for him was tortuous with many twists and turns because of the resistance of some people, the plotting of the leaders against him, and the lack of fidelity by most of his followers. When Jesus was lifted up on the cross, all of those realities were lifted up with him. He was at the summit, and all the efforts to get there were with him at that moment. That is the meaning of saying that all the events of the life of Jesus are fulfilled, caught up, gathered together in his death and resurrection. Everything he had to endure was worthwhile not only for him but especially for us.

And so no matter what the event in the life of Jesus may be that we are celebrating, we do so within the Mass. All is contained in the Eucharist since all is contained in Christ's paschal mystery.

The Spiral

The liturgical year is a cycle, a circle of events which are repeated annually. A problem with this truth is that if you go around in circles, you do not get anywhere. The ninth beatitude, they say, is, "Blessed are they who go around in circles for they shall be called big wheels." That sounds pretty negative, but the truth is that by celebrating the liturgical year we are getting somewhere; we are making progress. Each liturgical year builds on the previous one to form a spiral which is ever ascending toward heaven. With each year we progress closer to that moment when Jesus will come again in glory. Every liturgical celebration adds meaning to our prayer: "Protect us from all anxiety as we wait in joyful hope for the coming of our Savior, Jesus Christ."

---

[8] The names, "September, October, November, and December" are derived from Latin and indicate the seventh, eighth, ninth, and tenth months.

But where do we begin our annual counting of time? January is completely arbitrary, and the names of the last four months of the year let us know that at one time we began the year in March, the month in which the first day of spring always occurs.[8] Spring is a time of awakening and seems to be the time to begin the secular year, and some even think we should begin the liturgical year with Lent when we prepare to celebrate our great spring festival of Easter. The conciliar commission which was charged with arranging the Sacramentary and the Lectionary debated the issue. The outcome, perhaps I should say compromise, was to settle on the First Sunday of Advent as the inauguration of the liturgical year.

Whenever we begin the year, there is a tension between a thematic arrangement of feasts and a chronological one. This is what I mean. We celebrate the birth of Jesus on December 25. We celebrate his conception nine months previously on March 25, which always occurs during Lent. The result is that we turn our thoughts to the conception of Jesus by a chronological reckoning when we are preparing to celebrate his paschal mystery according to our thematic arrangement. Equally we conclude the Christmas season with the Baptism of the Lord as an adult two Sundays after Christmas, but forty days after Christmas we celebrate his Presentation as an infant in the temple. If this tension is an obstacle, it is not an insurmountable one. We must recognize that the liturgical year is not a dramatic reenactment of the life of Jesus. It is a mystical entering into the events of our salvation.

Mary and the Saints

The liturgical year is a celebration of Christ, that is, of Jesus who has been exalted through his death and resurrection as Lord and Christ, as the Head of his Body, the Church from which he cannot be separated. To celebrate Christ is to celebrate both Head and members. The liturgical year, therefore, includes Mary and the other saints. The *Constitution on the Sacred Liturgy* is simple and clear: "In celebrating the annual cycle of Christ's mysteries, the Church honors with special love the Blessed Mary, Mother of God, who is joined by an inseparable bond to the saving work of her son…. The Church has also included in the annual cycle days devoted to the memory of the martyrs and the other saints. By celebrating the passage of these saints from earth to heaven the Church proclaims the paschal mystery as achieved in the saints who have suffered and been glorified with Christ."[9]

And yet the *Constitution on the Sacred Liturgy* admonishes us that "the minds of the faithful must be directed primarily toward the feasts of the Lord in which the mysteries of salvation are celebrated in the course of the year."[10]

To the unfolding of these mysteries we turn our attention in the following chapters.

---

[9] *Constitution on the Sacred Liturgy*, nos. 103 and 104.
[10] *Ibid.*, no. 108.

Chapter 6

Advent, Christmas, Epiphany

"The Word became flesh and made his dwelling among us."
(John 1:14)

W̲ᴇ ꜱᴀʏ ᴛʜᴀᴛ ᴛɪᴍᴇ ʜᴇᴀʟꜱ all wounds, that time will tell, and
that time waits for no man. Actually time does nothing, but it
is the necessary context in which we live out our lives. Cardinal Henry Edward Manning wrote in his book, *The Eternal Priesthood*: "Time is so precious that God gives it to us only moment
by moment, and he never gives a single moment without taking the previous moment away."

We use our precious time well when we participate in the
saving events of the life of Jesus by means of our liturgical celebrations. We do not begin the liturgical year with creation, so
that we do not read from Genesis 1:1: "In the beginning God
created the heavens and the earth"; rather we begin with the
re-creation, and so we read from John 1:1: "In the beginning was
the Word... and the Word became flesh." The awesomeness of
the incarnation of the Son of God compels us not only to celebrate his coming into our world at Christmas, but to devote
four weeks to preparing for that festival. By a devout attention
to the inspired word of God during Advent we prepare to receive the incarnate Word of God at Christmas.

73

The foundation for our Advent was laid at Rome during the sixth century as a joyful preparation for Christmas. Elsewhere a period of ascetical practices had been initiated earlier. Eventually the more penitential character of the Gallican Advent in particular spread its influence, and the Roman liturgical Advent took on an ambivalent nature as could be seen in the retention of "Alleluia," a song of joy, together with the use of violet vestments, a sign of penance.

The liturgical reform directed by Vatican II restored Advent to a time, not of penance, but of joyful expectation since the anticipation of a joyful event should itself be joyful. Although the "Gloria" is not part of Sunday Masses during Advent, it is omitted not because we are to be sad or sorrowful, but only so that on Christmas our singing of this great song may in a certain way be a new experience for us.[1] Somewhat disconcertingly the violet vestments have been retained, and no official explanation of their continued use has been forthcoming. Some favor purple, rather than violet, during Advent. [Both violet and purple are mixtures of blue and red. In violet the blue dominates to produce a dark shade, and in purple the red dominates to produce a brighter shade.] Still others urge the use of blue vestments which would both obviate the impression that Advent is a kind of mini-Lent and would direct attention to Mary during what can be considered a Marian season. The National Conference of Bishops are empowered to make a decision in this matter.[2]

---

[1] See the restored *Calendarium Romanum*, page 61.

[2] See the General Instruction of the *Roman Missal*, no. 308. All citations are from the 4th edition. Actually the Conference is to make proposals to the Holy See, but the matter is merely disciplinary and even a diocesan Bishop should be able to determine such a simple matter as the color of vestments in his own diocese.

The season of Advent was instituted to prepare for the celebration of the birth of Jesus Christ, but it soon took on an eschatological sense as well. And so our Advent is a preparation both for the first coming of Christ into our world and for his second coming at the end of time. The great Abbot Columba Marmion even spoke of three Advents or comings of God's Son: from the bosom of the Father in eternity, from the womb of Mary at Christmas, and from heaven in the second coming at the end of time.[3] The liturgy, perhaps unfortunately, pays but scant attention to the eternal generation of the Son. From the First Sunday of Advent through December 16 the emphasis is on the second coming; from December 17 through December 24 the emphasis turns to the first coming of Christ in his birth. The two Prefaces of Advent reflect the two themes, but it should be remembered that this is a matter of emphasis only, not of exclusiveness. The two themes tend to intermingle in the readings and prayers throughout the entire season.

Advent stands somewhere between the two comings of Christ. Its joyful celebration reflects the meaning of Christian living as it enables us to share in the salvific coming of Christ in history so that his future coming may one day be a reality. The liturgical readings from the Old Testament help us to develop a sincere spirit of longing and expectation while the gospels gradually unfold the meaning of his incarnation and life among us.

---

[3] See his excellent book, *Christ in His Mysteries.*

The Sundays of Advent

The scripture readings for the Sundays of Advent are on a three year cycle. In all three the first Sunday presents an eschatological theme. This means that we begin the liturgical year by concentrating on its conclusion when Christ will come again. Some TV evangelists proclaim the end of the world as a dreadful time of doom and destruction. In contrast the Second Letter of Peter states: "What we await are new heavens and a new earth where, according to his promise, the justice of God will reside."[4] Taking its inspiration from this letter and other scriptures, the Second Vatican Council declared: "We do not know the time for the consummation of the earth and of humanity. Nor do we know how all things will be transformed. As deformed by sin, the shape of this world will pass away, but we are taught that God is preparing a new dwelling place and a new earth where justice abides, and whose blessedness will answer and surpass all the longings for peace which spring up in the human heart."[5] The universe will one day come to an end but only in the sense that the construction of a building comes to an end. When a building is finished, it does not cease to exist; rather, its development has been completed and it is ready to fulfill its purpose. It is in that sense that the universe one day will be finished. Exactly how that will happen, or even what that fully means, we do not know, but in faith we await the coming of Christ to bring all things to completion so that he may present to his Father the kingdom in all its glory.

---

[4] 2 Peter 3:13. See also Acts 3:21, Romans 3:19ff., and Revelation 21:1.
[5] *Pastoral Constitution on the Church in the Modern World*, no. 39.

In the First Preface of Advent we say: "Now we watch for the day, hoping that the salvation promised us will be ours when Christ our Lord will come again in his glory." In every Mass after the Our Father we pray: "…protect us all from all anxiety as we wait in joyful hope for the coming of our Savior, Jesus Christ." It is this doctrine of the end times which is celebrated on the First Sunday of Advent.

The gospels for the Second and Third Sundays of all three cycles feature St. John the Baptist. Frankly it is a little difficult to determine the exact meaning of this emphasis since John's admonitions seem more suited to Lent than to Advent. Some find meaning in relating his message to the eschatological theme of the First Sunday. Others insist that observing the witness of the Baptist reminds us that Jesus accomplished his mission as an adult who suffered, died, and rose from the dead rather than as an appealing infant asleep in the manger.

The Fourth Sundays in all three cycles turn our attention to preparing for the birth of Jesus. In the A cycle St. Matthew tells us "how the birth of Jesus Christ came about." He recounts the touching story of St. Joseph who was so humble that he feared to become part of what seemed to him to be a very great mystery when he found Mary to be with child by the power of the Holy Spirit. The angel assured him that he should be without fear. In God's eyes Joseph was that just man, that wise and loyal servant whom he placed at the head of God's family so that with a husband's love he might cherish Mary and with fatherly care watch over Jesus Christ, God's own Son.[6]

In the B cycle St. Luke relates the remarkable event in which the Angel Gabriel announced to Mary that she would

---

[6] See Preface 62 for Joseph, Husband of Mary.

conceive and bear a son whose "name would be Jesus and who would be called Son of God." This gospel marks the beginning of Christian salvation history. In the C cycle St. Luke tells us how Mary, thinking not of herself but only of Elizabeth, went with haste to help her relative who had become pregnant in her old age. Mary did what we all may do, which is to bring Christ to others. The Fourth Sunday in each cycle leads us directly to the awesome and wonderful event of the birth of God's Son into our world.

The season of Advent is four weeks long — but only approximately. When Christmas falls on a Monday, we have an Advent of only twenty-two days. When Christmas falls on a Sunday, we have an Advent of a full four weeks. Most of us seem to love Advent and that is one reason for wanting it to be as long as possible. There is a distinct pleasure in looking forward to Christmas. Advent, as we have seen, is also a season of expectation for Christ's return at the end of time. Then Christ will turn the universal kingdom over to his Father for his honor and glory. The Church has already waited a long while for that return, and so a lengthy Advent seems appropriate.

I confess to a vague feeling that the period of the Old Testament was much longer than the time of the New Testament. The fact is that the era from the time of the birth of Christ until the present is now longer than the era from the call of Abraham in the Old Testament until the first Christmas (Abraham is dated around 1800 years before Christ). But just where are we in the history of the Church and the world? Are we almost at its end? Are we actually still only at the beginning of our history so that possibly Catholics living in the sixty-first century will say of us living in the twenty-first century, "How blessed they were to have lived so close to the time of Christ and his apostles." Who knows? Jesus himself said, "As for the exact day or hour, no one knows, neither the angels in heaven nor the Son, but the Father only." And yet the truth that Christ will come again is part of our faith. It is right that we look forward to the fulfillment of the first coming of Christ in his second coming. We ought to yearn for the day of the general resurrection when Christ will hand over the kingdom to his Father.[7] In Advent we should pray for the virtue of hope, a confident trust that at the second coming all wrongs will be righted, justice will be done, and peace will prevail — all to the greater honor and glory of God.

The Advent Solemnities

The Solemnity of the Immaculate Conception of Mary always falls within Advent, on December 8, and quite appropriately since Mary was immaculately conceived for the sake of that moment when the Son of God was conceived in her womb. Our celebration of December 8 is incomplete until our celebration of March 25. The one leads to the other. March 25, it must be remembered, is not a feast of Mary but a feast of Jesus. The annunciation is that moment when the human life of Jesus began in Mary's womb. The Solemnity of the Annunciation, even though it most frequently occurs during Lent, is actually an Advent celebration. It marks the beginning of Mary's nine months of waiting and preparing for the birth of her child. Of course we suffer some confusion since March 25 is determined by the length of human gestation and the observances of Ad-

---

[7] See 1 Corinthians 15:24.

vent are arranged thematically. Be that as it may, both the Solemnity of the Immaculate Conception and that of the Annunciation look forward to that great day which we call Christmas.

An Advent Saint

The liturgy of the Second and Third Sundays of Advent feature St. John the Baptist. For many people, however, the saint who is most closely connected with Christmas, after Mary and Joseph, is not John the Baptist. It is St. Nicholas.

Jolly St. Nick in his bright red suit presents quite a contrast with the austerity of the Baptist who was clothed in camel's hair and wore a leather belt around his waist. Even so, St. Nicholas can serve as part of our Advent preparations. He was a fourth century bishop of Myra in Lycia (which is now part of Turkey). A popular story about him revolves around a poor man who could not provide dowries for his three daughters. As each girl reached marriageable age, Nicholas secretly left a bag of gold for the father so that he could arrange the weddings. Over the centuries Nicholas became a symbol of the gift-giving which is part of the celebration of Christmas.

This bishop's name is Greek ("Nikelaos"). The first part of his name, "Nike," means "victory." It is the name that was given to the Greek goddess of victory. Our government has employed it to designate a missile, and a sporting goods company has used it for its products. We should associate it with Christ. Some representations of Christ the King place this word, "Nike," beneath his feet to remind us that Christ has won the victory over the selfishness of sin and the finality of death, and has been exalted as King of the universe.

But there is a second part to the name; it is "laos" which means "people" (it is the Greek word from which we have derived our word for the baptized, the "lay" people.) This meaning should help us recognize that the great victory of Christ was for the benefit of his people. He did it all for us in the greatest act of generous giving the world has ever seen.

The legends about the goodness and gift-giving of St. Nicholas have been symbolized in the Dutch version of his name, Santa Claus. His name represents some of the most delightful experiences of childhood, but even for adults it suggests jolliness and good-natured generosity and a man clothed in a bright red suit rather than camel's hair. But Santa Claus does not push the Baptist aside during Advent. By his preaching John hoped to move people away from the basis of sin, which is self-centeredness. Santa Claus symbolizes unselfishness. He represents what the Baptist intended to accomplish. He is the gift-giver who never receives a gift in return. Behind all the legends of good St. Nick is a yearning for a manifestation in a human person of the unselfish goodness which the eternal Son of God brought to our world. Even people who have no faith of any kind instinctively long for a sign of the generous love which Jesus both proclaimed and lived. That's why they love Santa Claus.

Preparing for Christmas means trying to become what Santa Claus represents, a personification of the kingdom of Christ. We are imbued with the Christmas spirit when indifference is turned into justice, when hatred is overcome by love, and when violence gives way to peace. Is there a Santa Claus? Of course. He is found in every person who shares in Christ's victory over sin.

The Celebration of Christmas

Christmas was late in becoming a yearly liturgical celebration. Its first appearance seems to have been at Rome in the year 336. The early Church was so occupied with the marvel of the paschal mystery that it did not as yet have room in its mind and heart for any other aspect of the life of Jesus among us. The Church saw clearly that its obligation to obey the commandment of Christ, "Do this in memory of Me," was fulfilled in continuous attention to his death and resurrection.

The observance of December 25th is so firmly fixed in our minds and hearts that I suspect we could not even imagine having Christmas at any other time. The fact is, however, that we really do not know on what day Jesus was born. The Bible is silent about the date. It was a decision of the Church to designate December 25th as the birthday of the Lord. This is how that decision came about.

In the year 274 A.D. the Roman Emperor Aurelian introduced the pagan feast of "The Birth of the Unconquered Sun" (in Latin, *Natalis Solis Invicti*), to be observed on December 25th, which in the Roman calendar was the date of the winter solstice. In autumn there is gradually less daylight until this solstice, which is the shortest day of the year in the northern hemisphere. The pagan Romans thought of the sun as seeming to die during the darkening days of autumn, but on the solstice they looked upon the sun as being "born again," since from that time the amount of daylight begins to increase.

By at least the year 336 the Church at Rome began to celebrate the birth of Christ on December 25th. The Church had been granted its freedom by the Emperor Constantine in 313. Persecutions ended and the Church set about to Christianize society. One of its first moves was "to baptize" the pagan feast of the birth of the sun. The winter solstice became Christmas. Our calendar has been corrected so that the winter solstice occurs on either December 21 or 22, depending on the year. But the symbolism remains. Christmas is our feast of light. In English we even have a pun. The birth of the sun has become the birth of the Son. The created sun has given way to its Creator.

The first reading at midnight Mass from the prophet Isaiah begins, "The people who walked in darkness have seen a great light." St. John in his gospel (1:5) confirms that the Son of God is the light which shines in the darkness and which the darkness does not overcome. Sin does not conquer Christ; Christ destroys sin.

It was a long, dark night from the first sin until the bright day of Christ. His coming was like the sun rising in the morning with fresh brilliance. Now the light of Christ brightens our minds with God's truth and warms our hearts with his love.

No matter how bleak our days may be, we should look to the future with hope because of the renewal of Christ's coming in our liturgical celebration. Christmas is a feast of light. Candles, Christmas tree bulbs, even the lights in our homes and on our streets ought to remind us that Jesus is the true light who comes into our world. Should we neglect or minimize Christmas? Bah! Humbug!

The Three Masses of Christmas

Our practice of celebrating three Masses on Christmas at midnight, at dawn, and during the day seems to have been derived from the fact that the Pope celebrated Mass at three stational churches in honor of the birth of Christ: at St. Peter's, at St. Mary Major, and St. Anastasia's. Some want to see in the three Masses a symbol of the threefold coming of Christ. The first Mass, celebrated within the mysterious darkness of midnight, suggests that profound mystery whereby the Son comes forth from the Father, begotten by him in eternity. The Mass at dawn is taken to represent the birth at Bethlehem, that Jesus as he is born from Mary is the light coming into our world. The Mass during day, the time of bright daylight, seems symbolic of the coming of Christ in glory at the end of time. These symbolisms are not a bad idea except that they are not supported by the scriptural texts of the three Masses. It seems better to concentrate in all three Masses on the birth of Jesus at Bethlehem.

Many a priest has been hard put to preach a Christmas homily on the Prologue of St. John's gospel at the Mass During the Day. There is a rubric in the Lectionary which suggests that the texts of the Vigil Mass on the afternoon of December 24 and those of the Masses of Christmas are interchangeable according to pastoral need. I personally find it helpful to combine the gospels from midnight and dawn for a more complete picture of what we are celebrating.

We focus on an infant, born in a little town in Judea which was nothing more than a insignificant outpost of the mighty Roman Empire. And yet we recognize that this birth changed all of history and gave a new meaning and purpose to our lives. Despite the humble appearances, we believe that in Bethlehem the Eternal Son of God was born of the Virgin Mary.

The appeal of Christmas is not so much the truth that God entered our world and that divinity took on humanity, but the manner in which this was done. God could have become human as a full grown adult with a great display of power and majesty. Instead he chose to come amid the most humble of circumstances, born of a simple girl of Nazareth whose spouse could not even find a place for them to stay in their ancestral city.

We know the story well. For most of us it has been part of our Christmas celebration from the time we could kneel as a child before the crib of an infant. Is there anything more God could have done to invite us to embrace him in love than to come to us as Jesus did at Bethlehem?

The meaning of Christmas is so simply profound that our recognition of it overflows from human thought and seeps into our deepest emotions. The significance of Christmas is more felt than understood. In the early nineteenth century an event occurred in the village of Oberndorf in Austria which led to an expression of the meaning of Christmas which people will probably cherish as long as this world endures.

A few days before Christmas in 1818 the organ in the church of St. Nicola broke down. It became clear that it was impossible to make repairs in time for the midnight Mass. The organist asked the parish priest, Father Josef Mohr, for permission to use a guitar at the Mass. He explained that they would keep the music simple but they did need some form of accompaniment. Father Mohr agreed and mentioned that he had been working on a Christmas poem, one which his people could understand, for they were without much education as were the shepherds who were invited to the crib in Bethlehem. The priest handed him a piece of paper on which he had written a text which came to only twenty-six words in German. There was no title to the brief poem.

The organist went to work. Shortly before Christmas, Franz Gruber had completed his melody. At midnight Mass in the church of St. Nicola in an Austrian village in the year 1818 people for the first time sang "Silent Night."

The carol needed no title. It had captured the spirit the feeling of Christmas. It was simple, humble, actually a lullaby to the Son of God. From Oberndorf in Austria it spread throughout the world and every Christmas it is sung in almost every language of the world by people of the Christian faith. A German carol became universal because a Jewish baby, the eternal Son of God, was born in Bethlehem as our Savior.

Christmas Continues

Christmas and Easter are now the only two Solemnities with an octave. The meaning of an octave is that an event is celebrated throughout eight days as one day. The Sunday within the octave is the Feast of the Holy Family (or Dec. 30 if Christmas falls on a Sunday). This lovely feast, instituted in 1921 by Pope Benedict XV, remembers that the Son of God became truly human, that within a family he grew in wisdom and age and favor before God and his people. Appropriate to a reflection on this feast is the beautiful and profound teaching of the Second Vatican Council in its *Pastoral Constitution on the Church in the Modern World*: "By his incarnation and birth the Son of God has united himself with every human person. He worked with human hands, he thought with a human mind, he acted by human choice, and he loved with a human heart. Born of the Virgin Mary, he has become one of us, like us in all things but sin. He has shown us the way and if we follow it, life and death are made holy and take on a whole new meaning."[8]

---

[8] *Pastoral Constitution on the Church in the Modern World*, no. 22.

Within the octave we observe the Feast of the Holy Innocents. The pro-life movement has adopted this day to commemorate the untold number of babies who have been aborted and to pray for an end to this wanton destruction of human life. The Octave Day of Christmas is complex. In the previous liturgy this day was the day of the circumcision of the Lord when he was given the name of Jesus. Now it is the Solemnity of Mary, the Mother of God, as well as World Day of Prayer for Peace. If that is not enough, it is also New Year's Day. However we approach it, we must not forget that we are celebrating the birth of Jesus.

The Epiphany

"Epiphany" means "manifestation" or "revelation." At one time, and still in some parts of the Church, January 6 is Christmas. I can remember that my parents referred to it as "Little Christmas." Our liturgical observance of Epiphany encompasses three events: the coming of the Magi, the baptism of Jesus in the Jordan, and the marriage feast at Cana. The reason the three are united is that each is a manifestation of Jesus as the Savior.

The first event, the coming of the Magi which we usually term simply the Epiphany, shows that Jesus came as the Savior for everyone. The significance of the Magi lies not in who they were but in who they were not. They were not Jews, and yet they too were invited to embrace the Savior. The gifts of the Magi have been given several interpretations but they all are taken to manifest something about Jesus, such as gold for his kingship, frankincense for his priesthood, and myrrh for his victimhood.

The second event, the baptism of the Lord, posed something of a problem for the early Church. How could Jesus, innocent and without sin, be baptized by John for the remission of sins? St. Paul gave a bold explanation: "God made him who did not know sin to be sin so that we might become the very holiness of God."[9] The baptism of the Lord not only reveals that Jesus overcame sins by accepting their burden, but more significantly it reveals that Jesus is the Son of God: "This is my beloved Son. My favor rests on him."[10] It is the Son of God who is our Savior by overcoming sin.

The third event is the marriage feat at Cana. "Jesus performed this first of his signs at Cana in Galilee. Thus did he *reveal* his glory, and his disciples began to believe in him."[11] The glory revealed is the new covenant. The wedding context symbolizes the new covenant relationship between God and his people. It is the era of abundance, symbolized by the great amount of wine which Jesus made from water. It is the new and better covenant, the choice wine which had been kept until that moment.

The three aspects of the Epiphany, the manifestation or revelation of Jesus, fit together this way: Jesus became the Savior of all men and women (Epiphany) by overcoming sins which he took upon himself (Baptism) and by establishing the new covenant of his blood, the new and everlasting covenant, the marriage covenant between God and his people (Cana). The antiphon for the Canticle of Mary at Evening Prayer in the Liturgy of the Hours sees all three manifestation as one celebration: "Three mysteries mark this holy day: today the star leads the Magi to the infant Christ; today water is changed into wine

---

[9] 2 Corinthians 5:21.
[10] Matthew 3:17.
[11] John 2:11.

for the wedding feast; today Christ wills to be baptized by John in the river Jordan to bring us salvation." The antiphon for the Canticle of Zechariah at Morning Prayer is more explanatory: "Today the Bridegroom claims his bride, the Church, since Christ has washed her sins away in Jordan's waters; the Magi hasten with their gifts to the royal wedding; and the wedding guests rejoice, for Christ has changed water into wine, alleluia."

The gospel of the marriage feast of Cana appears only once every three years in the C cycle. This is a serious error since Cana is integral to the meaning of the Epiphany. That gospel should be read every year. There is further confusion in the Lectionary since this gospel is not presented until the Second Sunday of the Year but the liturgical books declare that the Christmas season ends with the Baptism of the Lord, which is the First Sunday. Earlier liturgies extended the Christmas season until the Feast of the Presentation of the Lord, forty days after his birth. We should return to that earlier design, especially since the Presentation is a still further revelation of Jesus as the Savior and could be considered another aspect of the Epiphany.

In any case we ought to see the pattern: preparation during Advent, celebration at Christmas, and manifestation in the Epiphany. We will see this same pattern in the Easter liturgy: preparation during Lent, celebration during the Triduum, and manifestation at Pentecost. I will refer again to the Epiphany in the next chapter in the treatment of Pentecost.

Christmas the Paschal Mystery

Some liturgists have been frustrated by the fact that for most Catholics Christmas, and not Easter, is the greatest celebration of the year, at least emotionally. One reason, quite frankly, is that the Easter bunny is no competition for Santa Claus, nor can Easter music, although glorious, arouse our feelings as do our Christmas songs and carols, both religious and secular. More profoundly, we all know what birth means but we have never experienced a resurrection.

The truth is that the infancy of Jesus is a prefigurement of his paschal mystery, as scripture scholars such as Father Raymond Brown, S.S., have lucidly pointed out. The infant Jesus, like his ancestors, was taken into Egypt so that he could experience the Exodus event of Israel in their Passover, their coming forth from Egypt to the promised land. It was a prelude to his own paschal mystery in which he would pass from death to life. More directly his presentation in the temple forty days after his birth, when as the firstborn he was offered to the Lord, was an anticipation of his offering on the cross. The infancy narratives of the gospels anticipate the paschal mystery of his death and resurrection.

Moreover it is clear that Jesus as the Son of God could never suffer and die in his divine nature. He was conceived and born of the Virgin Mary, he took on human nature like our own, precisely so that he could go "up to Jerusalem and suffer greatly from the elders, the chief priests, and the scribes, and be put to death and on the third day be raised."[12] I doubt that Christmas will ever surrender its emotional appeal to Easter but its meaning cannot be grasped without an understanding of the paschal mystery of the death and resurrection of Jesus. Christmas is for the sake of Easter.

To the great celebration of the Easter event we now turn our attention.

---

[12] Matthew 16:21.

Chapter 7

Lent, Easter, Pentecost

"It is the Passover of the Lord." (Exodus 11:11)

THE SACRED TRIDUUM, the holy three days, of the death, burial, and resurrection of Jesus are the epitome of all liturgical celebrations. If we understand the term "Easter" properly, we may substitute it for the term "triduum," and indeed for the entire season of fifty days from the day of the resurrection until Pentecost.

The date of Easter Sunday determines both when Lent begins on Ash Wednesday and when the Easter season concludes on Pentecost Sunday. In the early Church agreeing on that date was no easy matter. Bitter hostilities marked endless debates. At length the first of all the ecumenical councils, that of Nicea in the year 325, settled on this formula: Easter is the first Sunday following the first full moon after the vernal equinox. That means that Easter always follows the first day of spring (the vernal equinox) which can fall on March 21 or March 22, but only after the moon has become full. Jewish Passover begins the night of that full moon, which can occur on any day of the week. To put it all another way, Easter is the Sunday after Passover.

Fifty days after Easter is Pentecost and forty days before Easter is the beginning of Lent. A Wednesday, rather than a Sunday, marks the onset of Lent. This is how that came about.

Six weeks of Lent provide forty-two days, but Sundays were not counted since they were never days of fast and penance. That left only thirty-six days including the Triduum. The remaining four were made up by starting on Ash Wednesday. Actually we still do not have exactly forty days since in contemporary practice Lent ends with the Mass of Holy Thursday, the beginning of the triduum.

When George W. Bush was first thinking about running for President, he went out into the garden of his home to contemplate his future. In the distance he saw a shadowy figure. He went up to it and said, "You look like Moses!" The figure said, "I am Moses." Bush replied, "Good, I need to talk to you about running for President." Moses answered, "I will not talk with you. The last time I talked to a bush I spent forty years wandering in the desert."

For forty years Moses did so wander, and to meet the Lord he went up to the mountain for forty days, as later would Elijah. Earlier in the time of Noah it rained for forty days and forty nights. And so on with many other instances involving the number forty. Forty in the Bible is not a precise measure. It is not a mathematical number but a symbolic one. It marks a period a time within which God's work is accomplished. We have forty days of Lent because Jesus spent forty days in the desert to prepare himself for his public ministry which led to the paschal mystery of his death and resurrection.

The Sundays of Lent

The First Sunday of Lent in all three cycles presents the motive for Lent, the story of the forty days which Jesus spent in the desert and the subsequent temptations by Satan. The Second Sunday in all three cycles presents a foreshadowing of the resurrection, the story of the transfiguration. The Third, Fourth, and Fifth Sundays of each cycle present Lenten themes. These are the Sundays for the scrutinies in preparation for baptism.

The gospels of the A cycle are concerned with Christian initiation. This is in accord with the *Constitution on the Sacred Liturgy* which declared that Lent "recalls baptism or prepares for it."[1] The Third Sunday presents the dialogue between Jesus and the Samaritan woman at the well in which the discussion about water is a symbol of baptism, the water of which "becomes a fountain leaping up to provide eternal life." The gospel of the Second Sunday is the fascinating narrative of the man born blind whose gift of sight is a sign of the faith which comes to us in baptism. The Fifth Sunday tells of the raising of Lazarus from the dead, an image of our dying and rising with Christ in baptism. "Since these passages are very important in relation to Christian initiation they may also be used for year B and C, especially when candidates for baptism are present."[2] In fact, the first plan for the Lectionary was to have only one cycle of Sunday readings for Lent, but fortunately the opinion prevailed that the richness of Lent could not adequately be presented within a single cycle.

The *Constitution on the Sacred Liturgy*, besides indicating the relationship of Lent to Christian initiation, pointed out that Lent also "stresses a penitential spirit and readies the faithful for the celebration of the paschal mystery after a closer attention to the word of God and more ardent prayer."[3] The C cycle is con-

---

[1] *Constitution on the Sacred Liturgy*, no. 109.
[2] Introduction to the Lectionary, Chapter II, no. 13.
[3] *Constitution on the Sacred Liturgy*, no. 109.

cerned with the penitential spirit. In the gospel of the Third Sunday, Jesus draws a lesson of repentance from current events, which were Pilate's murder of some Galileans and a falling tower's killing of eighteen Jews in Siloam. Jesus rejected a judgment of these people but warned, "You will all come to a like end unless you begin to reform." The Fourth Sunday tells the incomparable story to which we give the incomplete and inadequate name, the parable of the prodigal son. The Fifth Sunday shows the compassion of Jesus toward the woman caught in adultery but also quotes him as saying, "From now on, avoid this sin."

The B cycle "readies the faithful for the celebration of the paschal mystery." The gospel of the Third Sunday occurs "as the Jewish Passover was near when Jesus went up to Jerusalem." There he declared, "Destroy this temple (his body) and in three days I will raise it up." On the Fourth Sunday "Jesus declared to Nicodemus: 'Just as Moses lifted up the serpent in the desert, so must the Son of man be lifted up.'" The Book of Numbers, to which this gospel alludes, states that Moses "mounted" a bronze serpent on a pole. That verb is changed in the gospel to "lifted up," a verb which can refer to the fact that Jesus was lifted up on the cross and that he was lifted up from the grave. In the gospel of the Fifth Sunday Jesus gives an analogy for the paschal mystery: "Unless the grain of wheat falls to the earth and dies, it remains just a grain of wheat; but if it dies, it produces much fruit." The fruit of the paschal mystery is the imparting of the life of Christ to us.

The Old Testament readings present elements of salvation history, beginning with readings from Genesis on the three First Sundays. Abraham, "our father in faith," is featured on the Second Sunday in each cycle and Moses on the Third Sundays. The Fourth Sundays in their respective cycles speak of David (A), the prophets in general (B), and the liturgical celebration of the Passover under Joshua (C). The Fifth Sundays in each cycle present the promise of a new covenant. The second reading from the New Testament each Sunday is related either to the gospel or to the Old Testament reading.

Holy Week, the Great Week

The sixth Sunday begins Holy Week, which in some traditions was called the Great Week. This Sunday is Passion Sunday, which may also be termed Palm Sunday since the liturgy commemorates the entry of Jesus into Jerusalem when the crowds came out to meet Jesus with palm branches in their hands. It is helpful to begin the liturgy at a place other than the church so that there can be a true procession from that place, which represents Bethphage on the Mount of Olives, to the church which represents Jerusalem. On this Sunday the Passion narrative is proclaimed from Matthew (A cycle), Mark (B cycle), and Luke (C cycle). By all means the long form should be followed in each instance so that the account of the Last Supper and the institution of the Eucharist may be included. Of course the passion gospel should be divided into parts. It is good to get as many people involved as possible; for example, rather than have one reader do all the parts other than that of Jesus and the narrator, it is desirable to have separate readers for each person who speaks during the narrative. There may also be some value in having a small group represent the crowd so that the assembly need not follow the proclamation in their missalettes but may listen attentively.

The gospel of Monday of Holy Week contains a somewhat

unusual reference to chronology by St. John. He tells the story of the woman who anointed the feet of Jesus but he notes that this took place six days before Passover, the tenth day of Nisan, when the lamb to be sacrificed for the Passover was to be selected from the flock. John sees the episode of the anointing as the selection of Jesus to be the paschal lamb. Tuesday and Wednesday of Holy Week are devoted to the betrayal by Judas and the denial by Peter. The early Church refused to forget or determined not to cover over the betrayal by Judas and the denial by Peter. The Church, it seems, was disheartened by Judas and dismayed by Peter, but the evangelists were quick to show the contrast between the despair of Judas and the repentance of Peter.

Holy Thursday is still part of Lent. It was a time for the reconciliation of public penitents who would receive communion at the Mass of the Lord's Supper. There was also before evening a Mass in which the bishop blessed the oils to be used in the sacraments. This Mass has been restored. The bishop is to concelebrate with his priests to manifest his union with them who extend his priesthood, particularly by means of the sacraments. For pastoral reasons the bishop may select another suitable day for this Mass. For those who go to Mass daily but cannot participate in the evening Mass (such would not infrequently be the case with urban elderly), the bishop may allow a Mass on Thursday in the morning but by no means should it be the Mass of the Lord's Supper. The Conference of Bishops should supply prayers and readings for a Lenten Mass since Thursday is part of Lent until the Evening Mass of the Lord's Supper. We must be careful not to slip back into the abuse before the reform of Pius XII when the Mass of the Lord's Supper was celebrated in the morning!

Beginning the Triduum

Lent concludes with the evening Mass of the Lord's Supper. At that time the Triduum begins and it continues until after Evening Prayer on Easter Sunday. The three days, the triduum, are Good Friday, Holy Saturday, and Easter Sunday. Thursday evening, when the sun has set, marks the beginning of Friday in liturgical reckoning (just as liturgically considered Sunday begins on Saturday evening).

On Thursday evening we celebrate the Lord's Last Supper. The Sacramentary indicates that the principal mysteries which are commemorated in this Mass are "the institution of the Eucharist, the institution of the priesthood, and Christ's commandment of love." The first reading from the Book of Exodus tells the story of the Passover both because the Supper took place on the night of the Passover commemoration and because Jesus became the new Passover. The second reading from First Corinthians is the most ancient written account of the institution of the Eucharist. In the gospel Jesus exemplifies his commandment of love by washing the feet of his disciples.

When people ask why we do not have a Mass on Good Friday, the answer is that we do have a Mass on Good Friday; it is celebrated on Thursday evening. It is imperative to link the institution of the Eucharist with Good Friday, indeed with the entire triduum. Jesus instituted the Eucharist as the sacrament of the paschal mystery of his death, burial, and resurrection. To think of the Eucharist merely as providing the real presence of Christ so that he may be properly adored is to fall back into grave errors of another era.

Some time ago I came across a simple plaque which I admired. It shows a loaf of bread and a glass of wine on a table.

The caption says: "Jesus of Nazareth requests the honor of your presence at a dinner to be given in his honor." I appreciate the noble simplicity of this plaque, which you too may have seen, but I would like to change one word. It is the very last word. Of the Eucharist Jesus did not say, "Do this in *honor* of me." He said, "Do this in *memory* of me." Jesus of Nazareth requests the honor of our presence at a dinner to be given in his memory.

Of course we honor Jesus at Mass. Ignoring him would be like ignoring the host who has invited you into his home. Jesus is truly present in the Blessed Sacrament and is worthy of our profound adoration. But the Mass is not benediction or a eucharistic devotion. The purpose is different.

On the night before he died, knowing that the hour had come for him to pass from this world to the next, Jesus left us the sacrament of his paschal mystery under the appearances of bread and wine, a sacrificial meal which is the living memorial of his death and resurrection whereby he would glorify his Father and win our salvation. The term "living memorial" indicates that the Eucharist does not merely recall the death of Jesus but makes it a reality among us. The Eucharist is not like a crucifix or a painting which makes us think of the death of Jesus. The Eucharist is the sacrament, the living reality, by means of which we participate in the sacrificial death of Jesus.

When I was growing up, prayer books encouraged us to look upon the body and blood of Christ, consecrated at the Mass, and say silently, "My Lord and My God." These words of the apostle Thomas reflect not only our faith but are an excellent sentiment. And yet this sentiment does not express the primary purpose for which Christ gave us the Eucharist. Now the Church invites us after the consecration to proclaim the mystery of faith: "Christ has died; Christ is risen; Christ will come again." Notice the dynamic character of all four proclamations. We proclaim: "Dying you destroyed our death; rising you restored our life...," and "When we eat this bread and drink this cup, we proclaim your death, Lord Jesus, until you come in glory," or "Lord, by your cross and resurrection you have set us free; you are the Savior of the world."

These proclamations contain sentiments appropriate to the Mass. Christ is present in the Mass in the very act of his paschal mystery, his death and his resurrection for the glory of the Father and for our salvation. That is the mystery of faith which Jesus wants us to remember and which we live in the Mass.

In every eucharistic prayer after the consecration, the words of the priest express the truth that the Mass is a living memorial of the paschal mystery. A simple example is found in the Second Eucharistic Prayer: "In *memory* of his death and resurrection we offer you, Father, this life-giving bread, this saving cup." The Mass is our opportunity to be faithful to the command of Christ: "Do this in memory of Me."

At this Mass enough bread is consecrated for communion at the Liturgy of Good Friday (still another sign of the link between this Mass and Good Friday). The Blessed Sacrament is then brought in procession to the place of reposition where the Lord is to be adored until midnight. This manner of recognition of the Real Presence establishes a balance in our understanding of the sacrament and provides a proper opportunity to act in accord with our faith-filled instinct to adore Christ in the sacrament.

Good Friday

As far as I have been able to ascertain, English is the only language which refers to the day on which Jesus died as "Good."

What an appropriate adjective that is. That day was so good for us that it won our salvation since we know that "Jesus by dying destroyed our death." There is no Mass during the day; it was celebrated, remember, on Thursday evening. The ritual of this day, though stark, is celebrated in red vestments as a sign of Jesus' martyrdom, his witness to the truth of the mercy and compassion of his Father.

After the people have assembled, the priest prostrates himself before the altar (so does the deacon, if there is one). This is a very ancient form of a penitential rite, a wordless expression of humility and penitence. (The only other time there is a prostration in our liturgy is during the rite of ordination.) Then the priest says a brief prayer and the Liturgy of the Word begins. The first reading from Isaiah is one of the "Songs" of the Suffering Servant of the Lord, a particularly beautiful and striking one. In the light of fuller revelation we readily see Jesus in this reading. The second reading is from Hebrews about the priesthood of Jesus. The gospel is the story of the passion according to John. The Liturgy of the Word concludes with the General Intercessions, a variation on our familiar form of the Prayer of the Faithful, which strive to include everyone just as Jesus opened his arms on the cross to embrace us all. Then follows the veneration of the cross and Holy Communion. Most parishes provide also an opportunity to make the Stations of the Cross on this day.

Holy Saturday

The second day of the triduum, Holy Saturday is, it seems to me, the least observed of the three days because it is the least understood. This is the day to commemorate the burial of Jesus. When Joseph of Aramathea and Nicodemus helped to take Jesus down from the cross, they had no doubt that he had died. Their only thought was to give him a proper burial in accord with Jewish custom. The significance of Holy Saturday is the fact that the death of Jesus was real. The Liturgy on this day is silent except for the praying of the Liturgy of the Hours. Piety should move us to spend some time, however difficult that may be, in quiet reflection, watching as it were at the tomb of Jesus, waiting in expectation for the time of the great vigil.

The Easter Vigil

On Holy Saturday night the liturgy begins with a service of light: the blessing of the fire and the lighting of the paschal candle. The prayer which the priest offers after the people have assembled is not only devout but instructional: "...on this most holy night, when our Lord Jesus Christ passed from death to life, the Church invites her children throughout the world to come together in vigil and prayer. This is the Passover of the Lord: if we honor the memory of his death and resurrection by hearing his word and celebrating his mysteries, then we may be confident that we shall share his victory over death and live with him for ever in God." That surely sums up the meaning of this night.

The meaning of the service of light becomes manifest when the congregation is led into the church by the paschal candle to acclamations of "Christ our Light. Thanks be to God." Then the Easter Proclamation is sung, often referred to by its first word in Latin, *Exsultet*. It serves well as a subject of contemplation. Very profound are its sentiments: the wedding of the Jewish Passover with that of Christ, the repetition of "This is the night" to reflect the liturgical "now," the enigmatic "O happy fault, O necessary sin of Adam which gained for us so great a Redeemer." (I sometimes wonder how effective the Exsultet is without a homily.)

Then the vigil in the proper sense begins since a vigil is a prolonged time of scripture reading and prayer, a devout period of watching and waiting. The priest says to the people: "Dear friends in Christ, we have begun our solemn vigil. Let us now listen attentively to the word of God, recalling how he saved his people throughout history and in the fullness of time sent his own Son to be our Redeemer." Those words indicate the purpose of the scriptural readings, to present us with a digest of what is called "salvation history." There are seven readings from the Old Testament and two from the New. The directive allows for a reduction of Old Testament readings to three, but the reading from Exodus 4 is never to be omitted. Many pastors feel that doing all nine readings makes the service too long, especially if there are to be many baptisms. Frankly a few of the selections are not clearly related to the purpose so that not much harm seems to be done by omitting them. And yet the directive strongly reminds us that "it must always be borne in mind that the reading of the word of God is the fundamental element of the Easter Vigil."

My suggestion is this. Include the first reading from Genesis about creation (it seems logical to start with that), the second about Abraham and Isaac (since it is so closely related to God the Father and Jesus), and the third about the passage through the Red Sea (since it may never be omitted). That fulfills the minimum requirement. Then think about giving a more complete picture by reading Hebrews 11. It is a marvelous summary of salvation history by recalling the people of salvation history. It concludes by saying: "Despite the fact that all of these were approved because of their faith, they did not obtain what had been promised. God had made a better plan, a plan which

included us. Without us, they were not to be made perfect."
These last two verses of chapter 11 provide a smooth transition
to the New Testament readings. Give it a try.
A homily follows the gospel, and then the liturgy of baptism begins. The full rite of Christian initiation which encompasses baptism, confirmation, and First Eucharist, when done properly, is among the most thrilling and uplifting experiences of liturgy. The Litany of Saints should add the names of the saints of those to be baptized. The litany symbolizes the union of the baptized with the people of the Church throughout history. As with the Exsultet, the prayers are both devotional and instructional.

The assembly should be involved throughout. Especially after the words, "I baptize you in the name of the Father and of the Son and of the Holy Spirit," let the whole assembly in each instance say or even sing a strong "Amen!" After the baptized have been robed in white, someone from the assembly may ask, "Who are these all robed in white?" And the priest may answer: "These are the ones who have washed their robes and made them white in the blood of the lamb."[4] All renew their baptismal promises. Some of the newly baptized may lead intentions during the Prayer of the Faithful in which they are participating for the first time as baptized faithful. The Liturgy of the Eucharist follows in which the newly baptized complete their initiation.

Easter During the Day

The third day of the triduum begins with the Eucharist on Saturday night and continues through Evening Prayer on Sun-

---

[4] See Revelation 7:13-14. This paragraph, of course, represents only my modest suggestions.

day. On Sunday at Mass everyone is invited to renew baptismal promises. Easter Sunday has traditionally been a day for dressing up in bright spring fashions. Although many various colors are part of modern attire, the liturgical color of Easter is white. Back on the Second Sunday of Lent we heard the story of the transfiguration of Jesus on the mountain. That event was a prelude, a kind of sneak preview, of Easter Sunday. When Jesus was transfigured on the mountain, his garments became dazzlingly white. St. Mark in his gospel adds that Jesus' garments became "whiter than the work of any bleacher could make them." The gospel for Easter Sunday tells us that the angel who announced the resurrection to the women was wearing a white robe.

White reflects all the visible rays of the spectrum. It can be said to contain all colors, and so is a symbol of fullness or completeness. Cloth must be bleached to become white; since that is a kind of purifying process, white is also a symbol of purity. These facts are important to us on Easter Sunday. The resurrected Jesus appeared in white. He had risen to a new life, a perfect life, a life of completeness. He had been transformed. When Jesus came forth from the womb of Mary, he was human like us in all things but sin. Then in his humanity he took on the ugly griminess of sin. Death was the bleach, the purifying agent. When Jesus came forth from the tomb robed in white, he showed us what one day we ourselves will be like. But we must go through a process similar to that through which Jesus passed. When we were baptized, God began the bleaching process. We died with Jesus to a life of sin and rose to a new life. As we have seen, the white robe of baptism is a sign of putting on Christ and his way of living. Baptism was our first sharing in the death and resurrection of Jesus.

One day we will die. Our casket may be covered with

flowers as a tribute from family and friends. But when the casket is wheeled into the church, any flowers are removed and a white cloth, the symbol of baptism, will be placed over the casket. Next to our casket will stand the paschal candle, the tall white candle which is the symbol of the Risen Lord.

When Martha and Mary were in distress over the death of their brother, Lazarus, Jesus declared, "I am the resurrection and the life." He had already promised that he would give the gift of his body and blood, as St. John recounts in the sixth chapter of his gospel. There St. John quotes Jesus as saying, "Whoever eats my flesh and drinks my blood has life everlasting and I will raise him up on the last day" (6:54). In Holy Communion we receive the glorified body and blood of the Lord, a pledge and promise of our own resurrection.

Easter is the greatest liturgical celebration of our faith. It is so great that one day, however grandly and solemnly observed, is not sufficient for this wonderful event. The eight days from Easter Sunday through the Second Sunday of Easter are the octave, eight days which form one great Easter day. Easter continues for fifty days, including the octave, from the Sunday of the Solemnity of the Resurrection through Pentecost Sunday. The Sundays of the Easter season are not counted as Sundays *after* Easter but as Sundays *of* Easter. The Easter season is the time for mystagogy, a word from the Greek which means "to lead into the mystery." One early tradition dedicated the octave of Easter, known as "the week of the white robes," to deeper instruction of the newly baptized so that they could enter more fully into the meaning of the paschal mystery which they experienced in their initiation on Saturday night. The thinking was (and maybe should still be) that people cannot understand the meaning of Christian initiation until they have experienced it.

The rite brings with it the grace to go more deeply into the instruction which was given during the catechumenate. The special time for mystagogy usually concluded with the Second Sunday of Easter, sometimes called in Latin *Dominica in Albis Deponendis*, the Sunday for laying aside the white robes. The spirit of mystagogy should pervade the Sunday celebration of the Eucharist throughout the Easter season for the benefit of all the faithful.

The Solemnity of the Ascension, forty days after Easter Sunday, reveals that Jesus rose from the dead, not to renew his mortal life, but to enter into the fullness of life as Lord and Christ, the Head of the Church, whom we are destined to follow into the glory of heaven. (Because forty in the Bible is symbolic and not a mathematical number, it is permitted by indult to celebrate the Ascension on the Seventh Sunday of Easter.) The Friday after the Ascension we begin the novena of prayer for a renewed coming of the Holy Spirit upon the Church at Pentecost. The Solemnity of Pentecost completes and concludes our fifty days of celebrating the paschal mystery, the death and resurrection of Christ. About Pentecost much more needs to be said.

The Solemnity of Pentecost

When people come to Mass on Easter Sunday or Christmas day, they have a clear perception of what the occasion is, even those who attend only once or twice a year. But on Pentecost? My informal, unscientific poll indicates that over two thirds of the people arrive at Mass on Pentecost thinking that it is just another Sunday. Pentecost is like a famous person who has even more famous relatives. In one sense Pentecost is overshadowed by its relative, Easter, but its significance can be appreciated by understanding its other renowned relatives, Christmas and Epiphany. Pentecost is to Easter what the Epiphany is to Christmas. Our celebration of the Epiphany manifests that Jesus, born of the house of David of the tribe of Judah, is the Messiah not only for the people from whom he was born through Mary in his humanity, but for all the people who will be born from him through water and the Holy Spirit. Epiphany is the revelation of God in Jesus Christ to the whole world.

Pentecost is an epiphany which reveals or manifests the meaning of Easter. In this sense "Easter" refers to the paschal mystery, the death and resurrection of Jesus. On Good Friday people looked up and saw an individual dying on the cross. On Easter Sunday some of the women and the other disciples saw an individual who had been raised from the dead. Pentecost reveals that seeing is not believing, that faith goes beyond what the eyes behold to perceive that Jesus in his death and resurrection, although seeming to be alone in both his agony and his glorification, is exalted by his heavenly Father as Lord and Christ, Savior of the world, and Head of the Church.

Pope Pius XII in 1943, reflecting the ancient patristic teachings and quoting Pope Leo XIII, wrote in his encyclical, *Mystici Corporis*: "The Church which, already conceived, came forth from the side of Christ in his death on the cross, first showed itself before the eyes of men on the great day of Pentecost."[5] After Jesus offered his life on the cross, he was exalted in his resurrection by his Father and he shared his life with his Church, his mystical body. This great truth was revealed at Pentecost.

---

[5] *Mystici Corporis*, no. 27.

It is important to recognize what Pentecost is not. First, even though people have heard the contrary many times, it is not the birthday of the Church. Of course, the expression, "birth of the Church," is only an analogy but its application to Pentecost is neither helpful nor appropriate. The origin of this popularization seems to have been catechetical but all patristic and papal teachings refer to Easter, the paschal mystery, as the birth of the Church and to Pentecost as its manifestation or epiphany. Affirming that traditional teaching, the Second Vatican Council stated: "From the side of Christ as he lay asleep on the cross was born that wonderful sacrament which is the Church in its entirety…. On the day of Pentecost the Church was manifested to the world."[6] (Can it be true that on a certain Pentecost Sunday the people were led in singing, "Happy birthday, dear Church, happy birthday to you"? I am afraid it is true. I was there to hear it.)

Pentecost belongs to the beginning of the Church's life as Epiphany belongs to the beginning of Jesus' life. The Solemnity of Pentecost completes Easter as the Solemnity of the Epiphany completes Christmas. In the Preface we proclaim to the Father: "Today you sent the Holy Spirit on those marked out to be your children by sharing the life of your only Son, and so you brought the paschal mystery to its completion." The word "Pentecost" is a number rather than a name. In Greek it means "fiftieth," and suggests that Pentecost does not stand on its own. It occurred fifty days after Passover and originally praised God for the wheat harvest. Later a commemoration of the Mosaic covenant was added to the observance. That is why there was

---

6   *Constitution on the Sacred Liturgy*, no. 5-6.

such a large number of pilgrims in Jerusalem when the Holy Spirit came. St. Luke's account in the Acts of the Apostles emphasizes that there were many people from many different places. After the day of Pentecost the Church by the power of the Holy Spirit spread to those places and beyond to the whole world. Pentecost celebrates the new and everlasting covenant, the Church, which was established in the blood of Christ. Jesus opened his arms on the cross to embrace the whole world, and he continues to open his arms through the Church. In the Preface we also proclaim, "Today we celebrate the great beginning of your Church when the Holy Spirit made known to all peoples the one true God, and created from the many languages of man one voice to proclaim one faith."

Recognizing that Easter, and not Pentecost, is the birth of the Church puts into proper light the practice of giving birth to members of the Church during the Easter Vigil through the sacraments of Christian initiation.

Secondly, it is important to note that Pentecost is not the feast of the Holy Spirit. To speak of Pentecost as the feast of the Holy Spirit tends to separate it from Easter of which it is the completion. More profoundly, all liturgical celebrations, even those which are designated as solemnities or feasts of the Lord or of the saints, are Trinitarian; they are celebrated through, with, and in Christ in the unity of the Holy Spirit for the honor and glory of the Father. The Trinity of Persons in God does not provide us with variety so that we can choose according to our taste the Person to whom we have devotion. The Persons of the Trinity are a family in which they are not only relatives of one another but in which they are the relationships themselves. Liturgical prayer is based on these relationships. Liturgical petition asks the Father to send the Holy Spirit through his Son.

Consider the Opening Prayer for the Solemnity of Pentecost: "God our Father, let the Spirit you sent on your Church to begin the teaching of the gospel continue to work in the world through the hearts of all who believe." Only hymns of late origin and prayers which are not rooted in liturgical tradition call upon the Holy Spirit directly. The Preface of the Mass expresses the fact that the liturgical thanksgiving of the eucharistic celebration praises the Father for sending the Holy Spirit through his Son upon the Church. The liturgy does not discriminate against the Holy Spirit; it simply prays in accord with God's revelation of himself to the Church.

At Pentecost we experience the Father's answer to our prayers. Together with his Son he sends the Holy Spirit anew. We should emphasize "anew." What sets Pentecost apart is the celebration of a specific mission of the Spirit. It is not as if the Holy Spirit remained hidden in the Trinity until Pentecost or that the Spirit was not at work until we received the trinitarian revelation. In the New Testament theology of St. John, for example, Jesus granted the gift of the Holy Spirit on the night of his resurrection: "He breathed on them and said, 'Receive the Holy Spirit. Whose sins you forgive are forgiven them, and whose sins you retain are retained.'"[7]

There is a sacramental parallel to Easter and Pentecost. As Easter is completed by Pentecost, so baptism is completed by confirmation. In 1971 Pope Paul VI in his *Apostolic Constitution on the Sacrament of Confirmation* wrote: "In fulfillment of Christ's wish the apostles imparted the gift of the Holy Spirit to the newly baptized by the laying on of hands to complete

---

[7] John 20:22-23.

the grace of baptism. This laying on of hands is rightly recognized by Catholic tradition as the beginning of the sacrament of confirmation, which in a certain way perpetuates the grace of Pentecost in the Church." The celebration of confirmation with baptism at the Easter Vigil reflects Johannine theology, and the celebration of confirmation at Pentecost reflects Lucan theology.

The Pentecostal mission of the Holy Spirit can be understood through the symbol of fire: "Tongues as of fire appeared which parted and came to rest on each of them. All were filled with the Holy Spirit."[8] Pentecostal fire does two things. It gives light and it gives warmth. The disciples were initially confused by the death of Jesus. Even after the resurrection they were not quite sure what it all meant and what they were to do. They needed the wisdom of the Holy Spirit to give them the light of faith. They also needed the love of the Holy Spirit to inflame their faith with the warmth of piety and zeal. Their enlightened faith and their loving zeal moved them to preach the gospel to manifest the Church. Because of this symbol of fire, red is the liturgical color of Pentecost. It is appropriate for the people to wear something red for the Mass on Pentecost Sunday. On the Sixth and Seventh Sundays of Easter an announcement may be made in this fashion: "Please wear something red to Mass on Pentecost Sunday. Red is a symbol of the fire of the Holy Spirit who gives us the light of faith and the warmth of love." When people follow this suggestion, the church on Pentecost seems aflame with the gift of the Holy Spirit.

Pentecost is so important that it is the occasion for the

---

[8] Acts 2:3.

original novena in the Church. The nine days between the Solemnity of the Ascension and that of Pentecost are days of intense prayer for the renewed coming of the Holy Spirit. During these days the apostles "devoted themselves with one accord to prayer, together with some women, and Mary the
mother of Jesus, and his brothers."[9] That prayer is reflected in
the Liturgy of the Hours for the days between the Ascension
and Pentecost but it does not reach into popular piety. A simple
novena can be constructed, however, from the intercessions at
Morning and Evening Prayer of the Liturgy of the Hours on these
days and prayed with the people before or after daily Mass, or,
as on any weekdays, the intercessions from Morning Prayer or
Evening Prayer may replace the customary general intercessions
at Mass.[10]

We will never, I suppose, be able to arouse sentiments
about Pentecost which are as intense as those most of us feel
for Christmas or Easter or even Epiphany. Actually we do not
have to make the effort to elicit something entirely different in
our piety since these solemnities are all relatives. They form a
family of feasts. Christmas is completed by Epiphany and leads
us to Easter, the paschal mystery, which is completed by Pentecost. If we do not make of Pentecost a forgotten relative, then
through our family of feast days we will all joyfully give thanks
and praise to God our Father through his Son in the unity of
the Holy Spirit.

---

[9] Acts 1:14.
[10] See General Instruction of the *Liturgy of the Hours*, no. 93.

Chapter 8

Sunday, Ordinary Time, and Weekdays

"Today is holy to the Lord your God. Do not be sad and do not weep." (Nehemiah 8:9)

Every Easter Sunday our churches are packed. People are there who have not seen the inside of a church since last Easter. Standing in the rear of an overcrowded church on Easter Sunday a "once a year Catholic" whispered to his wife, "You'd think the regulars would stay away just once a year to give us a chance." As I look from the altar to the congregation, I wonder where all these people are the rest of the year. A priest friend of mine calls them "the paschal lambs." I am careful, however, not to admonish or humiliate them. I am pleased that they come at least once a year, and maybe again at Christmas. That is better than not at all, even though I wish they and all Catholics could grasp the essential importance of Sunday Mass.

Mass is what we Catholics do on the Lord's Day. It has been so since the very beginning. The first disciples of Jesus were all Jewish. They went to the synagogue on Saturday, the Sabbath, for a form of the liturgy of the word: scripture readings, a sermon by the rabbi, and prayers. On Sunday evening — and they had to meet in the evening since Sunday was a work day — they gathered in someone's home for the celebration of the Eucharist to fulfill the command of Jesus, "Do this in memory of me." Pope John Paul II observed that "there have always been groups within Christianity which observe both the Sabbath and Sunday as 'two brother days.'"[1]

The Church spread beyond Judea northward into Syria and Gentiles began to become disciples. St. Luke notes in the Acts of the Apostles that "it was in Antioch (in Syria) that the disciples were called Christians for the first time."[2] St. Ignatius, the Bishop of Antioch, who died around 107 A.D., gave us the name "Catholic" to indicate that the Church is universal, that it embraces everyone without exception. The Catholic Christians in Antioch did not, of course, go to the synagogue, but when they met on Sunday evening for the Eucharist they heard some of the letters of St. Paul, which marked the beginning of the New Testament, and then later the gospels.

St. Justin, a layman, is an important witness to the practice at Rome in his time. He wrote around the year 150: "On Sunday we have a common assembly. The recollections of the apostles or the writings of the prophets are read. When the reader has finished, the presider speaks to us. Then we all stand and pray. After the prayer, bread and wine are brought forward. The presider offers prayers and gives thanks and the assembly express their assent by saying 'Amen.' The Eucharist is distributed, everyone communicates, and the deacons take it to those who are absent. We do not consume the eucharistic bread and wine as if they were ordinary food and drink for we have been

---

[1]   Apostolate Letter, *Dies Domini*, no. 23.
[2]   Acts 11:26.

taught that the food which our flesh and blood assimilates for its nourishment becomes the flesh and blood of the incarnate Jesus."[3]

This brief excerpt from St. Justin's writings bears witness that our Mass today is essentially the same as that of the Catholics at Rome in the middle of the second century. St. Justin adds this next important fact: "We hold our common assembly on Sunday because it is the first day of the week and on that day our Savior Jesus Christ rose from the dead. He was crucified on Friday and on Sunday he appeared to his apostles and disciples."

In the early centuries of the Church there was only one great celebration, that of the paschal mystery, the death and resurrection of Jesus, of which the Eucharist is the sacrament. That celebration occurred every Sunday. Only later did a special Sunday of each year, that of Easter, become the preeminent celebration of the paschal mystery. Pope John Paul II wrote that every Sunday "is Easter which returns week by week, celebrating Christ's victory over sin and death."[4] The Church was so preoccupied with the paschal mystery that there was no celebration of Christmas until the year 336. Even then, as now, the birth of Jesus was celebrated with the sacrament of his death and resurrection, the holy Eucharist.

Many things about the Church have changed over the centuries, but not the tradition which calls us to celebrate the Eucharist on Sunday. It is not surprising that the Second Vatican Council in its *Constitution on the Sacred Liturgy* emphasized the importance of Sunday Eucharist. The Fathers of the Council wrote: "By an apostolic tradition which took its origin from the

---

[3] See the Office of Readings for the Third Sunday of Easter.

[4] Apostolate Letter, *Dies Domini*, Introduction.

very day of Christ's resurrection, the Church celebrates the paschal mystery every Sunday. With good reason, then, Sunday is known as the Lord's day. On this day Christ's faithful should come together so that by hearing the word of God and taking part in the Eucharist, they may call to mind the passion, the resurrection, and the glorification of the Lord Jesus, and may offer thanks to God."[5]

Sunday is our special day for the Liturgy of the Mass. "Liturgy" is a Greek word which has been restored to our Catholic vocabulary since the time of the Second Vatican Council. It means "the work of the people." Students of physics may recognize in this Greek word the origin of the technical word, "erg," which is a measure of energy. When we come to Mass on Sunday, we must make sure that we exert energy, that we do not reduce the meaning of the word, "liturgy," to irony. The Church urges us to observe Sunday as a day of rest, not so that we may do nothing, but so that we may enter whole-heartedly into the celebration of the sacred liturgy. Our vigor during Mass should be at high measure.

Sunday Mass should be a joyful, energetic experience for us. The Mass is like an oasis in the midst of a busy, hectic, and sometimes hostile, world. But it should still be work. This work requires us to direct our attention to what we are doing and to put forth the effort necessary to do it properly. Coming to Mass is not like going to a movie or watching TV. Such entertainment is largely passive; we sit back and relax and expect to be entertained. At Mass we are not to let the priest and ministers do all the work. Everyone is called to that full, active participation which the nature of the liturgy demands.

---

[5] *Constitution on the Sacred Liturgy*, no. 106.

Before and after Mass the spirit of the Eucharist should pervade the whole day. The Fathers of the Council continued, "The Lord's day is the original feast day, and it should be proposed to the piety of the faithful and taught to them in such a way that it may become in fact a day of joy and of freedom from work." I must hasten to add that this emphasis on Sunday does not exclude a Saturday evening celebration since liturgically Sunday does not begin at midnight but at sunset on the previous day. Actually the Saturday evening observance should remind us that Sunday is so special that it is longer than the twenty-four hours of an ordinary weekday.

In our American society it is pretty difficult, if not at times impossible, to observe Sunday as a Sabbath, as a day of rest. Some people have to work on Sunday if they want to keep their job. Others really have no other time to shop or do chores around the house. The *Code of Canon Law* helps us to understand what we should be striving for: "On Sundays... the faithful are bound... to abstain from those labors and business concerns which impede the worship to be rendered to God, the joy which is proper to the Lord's Day, or the proper relaxation of mind and body."[6] We may quite appropriately apply to Sunday this exhortation from the Book of Nehemiah: "Today is holy to the Lord your God. Do not be sad and do not weep. Go, eat rich foods and drink sweet drinks, for today is holy to the Lord. Do not be saddened this day, for rejoicing in the Lord must be your strength."[7]

The point is we should see to it that Sunday is different from the other days of the week. The first way to do that is to

---

[6] Canon 1247.
[7] Nehemiah 8:9-11.

make Sunday Mass an absolute priority. The Letter to the Hebrews reminds us: "We should not absent ourselves from the assembly, as some do, but encourage one another."[8] Other activities ought to be planned to accommodate the Mass, not the other way around. Cardinal Mahony of Los Angeles in his excellent Pastoral Letter on Sunday Mass wrote: "In the early years of the Church, a bishop in Syria urged his fellow bishops to exhort the people to be faithful to the assembly of the Church. 'Let them,' he said, 'not fail to attend, but let them gather faithfully together. Let no one deprive the Church by staying away; if they do, they deprive the Body of Christ of one of its members.'"

A second thing to do is to read the scriptures of that Sunday's Mass before coming to church. Every home should have not only a Bible but also a Sunday Missal. We all ought to come to Mass knowing what the readings will be so that we may be better prepared to listen to them within the grace-filled moments of the Mass.

A third means of preparation is to read the newspaper, to turn on the radio, or to look at the news on TV so that we may bring the concerns and problems of others with us to become part of our prayer at Mass. When Pope John Paul II was asked, "What does the Pope pray for?", he answered by quoting the first sentence of Vatican II's *Constitution on the Church in the Modern World*: "The joys and the hopes, the sorrows and the anxieties of the people of this age, especially of those who are poor or in any way afflicted, are the joys and hopes, the sorrows and the anxieties of the followers of Christ."[9]

---

[8] Hebrews 10:25.
[9] From his book, *Crossing the Threshold of Hope*.

The fourth thing to do is to remind each other of the importance of the Mass by wearing our Sunday best. I live in Southern California where some people come to Mass in tee shirts and shorts. I would never dream of turning them away, but I do wish they could remember that when they go to a wedding they dress in a special way. The Mass is the great wedding feast of the Lamb of God and we should dress in accord with that truth. Clothing does not have be as formal as for a Hollywood premier, nor should anyone who possesses only simple attire be made to feel out of place. We simply should select the best we have.

Are we obliged to go to Mass on Sunday? Well, yes we are. The *Code of Canon Law* stipulates: "Sunday is to be observed as the foremost holy day of obligation in the universal Church. On Sundays the faithful are bound to participate in the Mass."[10] Sunday Mass is what we do as Catholics. A recent poll indicated that about half the Catholics in the United States attend Mass faithfully every Sunday. I do not know how accurate that estimate is (I personally have never been questioned for any kind of poll; have you?), but it can move us to ask why we should go to Mass every Sunday, apart from the obligation. Why not just stay home?

Some people say that they do not bother with church because they don't feel that they are missing anything. Others insist that they have a deeper sense of God when they are alone at the beach or in the mountains, or when they simply reflect quietly at home. I do not deny that these people really sense no lack in failing to come to church, or that they feel closer to God

---

[10] Canons 1246 and 1247.

elsewhere. But all Catholics, both those who are regular at church and those who are not, must take into consideration some very important truths.

Although God is present everywhere at all times, he has chosen to make the sacrifice of his Son a reality for us only through the celebration of the Eucharist, the Mass. The Eucharist is the sacrament of the death and resurrection of Jesus Christ, the paschal mystery. This mystery is the central event of all human history, and so the Eucharist is to be the central and indispensable act of our worship. Within this sacred celebration God the Father has chosen to nourish us spiritually through word and sacrament. Even though the scriptures can and should be read at home, they take on a special meaning within the Mass since "Christ himself speaks when the holy scriptures are read in the church." Above all God our Father gives us the gift of his Son's body and blood, a form of nourishment which cannot be found elsewhere.

The Church insists that nothing can take the place of liturgical prayer, especially the Mass. The Mass is of higher value than any form of private prayer, not only because it proclaims the word of God and celebrates the sacrament of the Eucharist, but also because it is the model and source of all authentically Christian prayer. Those who neglect the Mass can easily wander into a type of prayer which is not in harmony with the teachings of Christ and the tradition of his Church. They also run the risk of becoming mavericks, people who are out of touch with sound doctrine and sane practice. Jesus manifests himself as the way, the truth, and the life chiefly through the liturgy, which is the indispensable source of the true Christian spirit.

The Letter to the Hebrews gives this plea: "We should not absent ourselves from the assembly, as some do, but encourage one another."[11] Encouragement we all need but there is something further. Since we are the body of Christ, a part of the body is missing when Catholics skip Mass. It is tempting to say, "No one will miss me," but God misses us. An eight-year-old boy satisfied an assignment in religion class by writing the following: "You should always go to church on Sunday because it makes God happy, and if there's anybody you want to make happy, it's God. Don't skip church to do something you think will be more fun, like going to the beach. This is wrong! And besides, the sun doesn't come out at the beach until noon anyway."

Pope John Paul II wrote in his marvelous Apostolic Letter, *Dies Domini*: "All the faithful should be convinced that they cannot live their faith or share fully in the life of the Christian community unless they participate regularly in the Sunday eucharistic assembly. The Eucharist is the full realization of the worship which humanity owes to God, and it cannot be compared to any other religious experience."[12] Catholics who do not go to Mass on Sunday are like husbands and wives who do not live together; something essential is missing.

Balance in Prayer

As we think about prayer further I ask you to picture a dark, chilly, November evening. There is no sound except for the soft, regular breathing of a single person who sits in such stillness that he appears to be asleep. But in his mind he sees an

---

[11] Hebrews 10:25.
[12] Apostolic Letter, *Dies Domini*, no. 81.

image, impossible to describe or even imagine, which puts him into contact with God, and his heart is filled with love for his heavenly Father. This person is Jesus who spent whole nights in prayer. He is the model of what we all must do, at least from time to time, and that is to set ourselves apart from duties and distractions in order to be alone with God. But Jesus gives us another example. We observe him when he is twelve years of age accompanying his parents to the temple in Jerusalem for the Passover festivities. Later we watch him as he leads his disciples every Sabbath to the synagogue for worship. And we see him at the supper table on the night before he offered his life in sacrifice. There united with his apostles in prayer and song, he institutes the Eucharist, the celebration of which is the indispensable source of the true Christian spirit. This is Jesus, who became human like us in all things, and who dedicated body and soul, mind and spirit, to the worship of his Father. Jesus was a person of prayer.

Praying alone as if removed from this world was something Jesus had to do in order to express in a human way his eternal relationship with his Father, but it was not enough for him. Because Jesus became one of us, part of the human race, he joined his disciples in community worship. Praying alone is not enough for us. In the liturgy of the Church Jesus invites us to be united with him in prayer and song for the celebration of the Eucharist, the living memorial of his death and resurrection.

Some people think that the only way to pray is be alone with no disturbances from people and no distractions by music. When they come to Church they are distressed to find an atmosphere which does not fit their preferences. They need to grow in appreciation for community worship, the prayer of the family of God. On the other hand some people have to admit that the only time they pray is when they go to church on Sunday. They need to set some priorities in their lives in order to make time for personal prayer to God.

Every Sunday should be the high point of prayer for us. It is an opportunity for us to renew our own baptism when we became children of God, transformed according to the image of the Son.

Jesus invites all of us to follow his example in a life of prayer balanced between private devotion and community worship.

Because of his incarnation we have in Jesus not only a perfect model but a human being whom we can see and appreciate. His teaching is not some obscure doctrine proclaimed in the abstraction of words alone. Divine though he is from all eternity, in time he became human like us to show us how to live, how to love, and how to pray.

Solemnities of the Lord in Ordinary Time

The Solemnities of the Lord which are observed on Sundays of Ordinary Time are those of the Trinity, the Body and Blood of the Lord (*Corpus Christi*), and Christ the King. The Solemnity of the Sacred Heart is always on the Friday after Corpus Christi. The Sundays of Ordinary Time may be impeded by other Solemnities, such as All Saints on November 1, or by other Feasts of the Lord, such as the Presentation on February 2. The liturgy has often had to struggle to keep Sundays pure and unobstructed. Even after the reforms of Vatican II, we still need further efforts to avoid deleting Sunday liturgy in favor of Solemnities of saints, such as that of John the Baptist on June 24 or Saints Peter and Paul on January 29. I am willing to make exceptions for All Saints on November 1 or All Souls on November 2 since they are a necessary means to foster sound Catholic piety, but the primacy of Sunday must be safeguarded.

Ordinary Time

The theme for the Sundays of Ordinary Time is usually determined by the gospel. The first reading is chosen to support the gospel in some way, but the second is an independent, continuous reading from New Testament selections other than the gospels. The A cycle features the gospel of St. Matthew, the B cycle that of St. Mark, and the C cycle that of St. Luke. St. John's gospel is favored during the Easter season, and his sixth chapter fills out the B cycle since the gospel of St. Mark is short, only sixteen chapters. On weekdays the first reading is on a two year cycle, but the gospels are arranged in a single series. Unless a solemnity or feast occurs, the weekday readings are preferred to other selections.

Weekdays, a Tale of Two Masses

Shall I give in to the temptation and say it? Yes, I will. It was the best of Masses. It was the worst of Masses. Well, almost. Recently I went on an automobile trip with my brothers, one an exemplary priest who was ordained in 1939, the other a lay person, now a widower but a dedicated father and grandfather. Our first morning away we attended a weekday Mass at one of the California missions. The priest who presided at the Mass, I discovered later, had been ordained in 1960. When he came to the door, he invited us to stand and sing the hymn, "Praise to the Lord, the Almighty." The thirty or some people present sang without instrumental accompaniment but not without enthusiasm. The priest was assisted by a young woman who, after the opening prayer, proclaimed the first reading in a clear, understandable voice and led us in a sung "Alleluia" as an introduction to the gospel. Following the gospel, the priest gave a succinct, appropriate homily in less than three minutes. He invited us to share in the Prayer of the Faithful and the people responded with some seven or eight spontaneous petitions which manifested that they had learned to pray unselfishly for the needs of others.

We sang a eucharistic acclamation. We stood throughout the Communion Rite.[13] There was a brief, but warm exchange of the sign of peace, and a few people went out of their way to greet my brothers and me. We received communion from hosts consecrated during that Mass and two ladies served as ministers of the cup. Following the concluding hymn many lingered in friendly conversation, and the priest waited at the door to bid everyone goodbye. The manner of celebration had been uplifting and devout. It was especially rewarding for my priest brother and me as old seminary professors to see the theory we have taught put into practice in a parish. My other brother, who attends daily Mass, said he wished they could have Mass like that every day back home. The people of the mission parish had said "yes" to the liturgical restoration of the Second Vatican Council.

During our vacation we also attended Mass at a parish

---

[13] The General Instruction of the *Roman Missal* calls for the people to stand throughout the Communion Rite until they have received when they may sit, no. 21.

church which will remain unidentified. The congregation was slightly larger than the one at the mission. It was a "no" Mass: no singing, no server, no lector, no homily, no prayer of the faithful, no sign of peace, no communion from the cup, and no hosts consecrated for us during the Mass.[14] I was relieved that there was also no collection. The priest, who seemed to be about the same age as my priest brother, recited the prayers in such a perfunctory fashion that I struggled to resist thinking of the admission of King Claudius in Shakespeare's *Hamlet*: "My words fly up, my thoughts remain below. Words without thoughts never to heaven go." I tried to overcome that temptation by concentrating on the principle, *ex opere operato*. The experience was discouraging and a real challenge to faith. The mission parish had worked at implementing the restored liturgy. The other parish had done nothing more than turn the altar around and employ English, but even that seemed half-hearted. It was almost as if the Second Vatican Council had not taken place.

In some places the restored liturgy, if I may adapt the words of G.K. Chesterton, has not been tried and been found wanting; it simply has not been tried. I do not suggest that a weekday Mass is to be as much like a Sunday celebration as possible. On the other hand to favor a "quiet" Mass as devotional is to fail to understand that the Mass by its nature is always a community celebration and does not, and actually cannot, fulfill our need for individual piety. The notion of a "private" Mass is a contradiction. The plea that on a weekday the Mass must be short because people have to get to work should not reduce us to a pre-Vatican II style liturgy. In fact, the people whose faith

---

[14] Despite the strongest official directives to the contrary, all the hosts were taken from the tabernacle.

moves them to come to Mass daily, or almost daily, deserve the best we can do.

To be brief we need not be superficial. All can be done expeditiously, but properly, especially the homily. A daily homily is not simply an abbreviated form of the Sunday homily. There is no need to try to harmonize the first reading and the gospel, or even to comment on each, since they are both continuous readings. In other words, the liturgy has not selected the first reading to reflect the theme of the gospel, as it does on Sundays. If neither reading readily suggests a topic, the homilist may comment on some other aspect of the liturgy, such as a part of the eucharistic prayer. On a saint's day a few words about the saint, without any attempt to apply the readings, are quite appropriate. Long preparation which involves consulting commentaries and homily aids is seldom practical for weekday Masses. The homily, which should not exceed two or three minutes, may be a reflection which is the fruit of the priest's meditation on the liturgy of the day. People who make the effort to participate in daily Mass deserve the effort it takes a priest to deliver a homily.

Singing may be simplified by selecting familiar favorites which can be sung from memory. Variety is not important at daily Mass. One stanza of an opening hymn is sufficient to unite the assembly and to stimulate alertness. It is very appropriate even on a weekday to sing the "Holy, Holy, Holy" and the eucharistic acclamation. The ideal of singing during communion admittedly presents the biggest difficulty but it is helpful if the people sing even briefly. We must be careful not to drift back into the old rite in which the priest did everything. Even at daily Mass it is important to have a server, a lector, and ministers of holy communion. These can easily be recruited from the regulars at daily Mass. They manifest that the Church is a community of various ministries whereby we serve one another.[15] The Prayer of the Faithful should not be omitted.[16] It is our response to the proclamation of the word: having heard the love of the Lord proclaimed in the readings, we are moved to pray that others will share in the Lord's love through our intercessions. The sign of peace prepares for Holy Communion. It is not optional, even at a daily Mass.[17] The Sacramentary can hardly be more emphatic about urging priests to communicate people from hosts consecrated at the Mass in which they participate, and to offer them the cup as well.[18]

The Pastoral Introduction to the revised Sacramentary includes the following points about weekday Mass:

1. The weekday Mass should enhance and never diminish the full and active participation of all those present. Though simpler than Sunday Mass, weekday Mass should involve a full complement of ministers.

2. Great importance should be attached to the use of music and singing even at weekday Mass.

3. A brief homily is strongly recommended.

---

[15] "The liturgy is the outstanding means by which the faithful can express in their lives and manifest to others the mystery of Christ and the real nature of the true Church" (*Constitution on the Sacred Liturgy*, no. 2).

[16] See no. 45 in the General Instruction of the *Roman Missal*.

[17] Some priests have been led to think that the sign of peace is optional because the Sacramentary states: "The deacon or the priest may add: Let us offer each other the sign of peace." What is optional is this exhortation; it may be omitted and the people then spontaneously offer the sign of peace. The Sacramentary clearly indicates that "all exchange an appropriate sign of peace."

[18] See the General Instruction of the *Roman Missal*, no. 56h, which states: "It is most important (the Latin is very strong: *valde optandum est*) that the faithful should receive the body of the Lord in hosts consecrated at the same Mass and should share the cup when it is permitted. Communion is thus a clearer sign of sharing in the sacrifice which is actually taking place."

4. The breaking of the bread takes on a special significance if smaller numbers permit all present to share in one bread; likewise it should be easy for everyone to share communion from the one cup.

The California mission church showed clearly that all of this can be done. The people and their priest made me think of the solemn declaration of the Second Vatican Council: "Zeal for the promotion and restoration of the liturgy is rightly held to be a sign of the providential disposition of God in our time, as a movement of the Holy Spirit in his Church. It is today a distinguishing mark of the Church's life, indeed of the whole tenor of contemporary religious thought and action."[19]

A Love for Daily Mass

Sunday was so prominent in the minds of the first disciples as the day of the Eucharist that it took a little while for the Church to develop the practice of daily Mass. At first Catholics prayed the psalms together as their weekday prayers, an observance which developed into the Divine Office, the Liturgy of the Hours, but as early as the era of St. Cyprian, who died in the year 258, there is evidence of a growing practice of celebrating the Eucharist on weekdays. By the early part of the fifth century, in the East St. John Chrysostom attested to the daily offering of Mass outside the season of Lent, and in the West St. Augustine showed that daily Mass had become usual. In one of his sermons St. Augustine told the candidates for baptism that they would hear the Lord's Prayer every day at Mass.

---

[19] *Constitution on the Sacred Liturgy*, no. 48.

Some restrictions were applied to the weekdays of Lent because of their penitential character. Since the Eucharist is always a joyful celebration, it was considered inappropriate to celebrate it each day during Lent. Slowly the understanding of both Lent and daily Mass developed so that toward the beginning of the eighth century under Pope Gregory II daily Mass during Lent became standard practice.

The celebration of Mass on Sunday ought to be of such beauty and significance that it should move us to yearn for the Mass and to wish to participate in it with a greater frequency than once a week. Weekday Masses should then in turn help us to grow in our enthusiasm for our Sunday celebration.

Innumerable saints have given the example of centering their entire lives on daily Mass. Father Josef Jungmann, S.J., one of the foremost liturgical scholars of the twentieth century, expressed a beautifully simple reason for daily Mass. He wrote in his classic work, *The Mass*, "Some people simply cannot stay away from what they love."[20]

---

[20] All of the data on daily Mass are taken from Father Jungmann's book.

Chapter 9

Mary and the Saints

*"I saw before me a huge crowd which no one could count from
every nation, race, people, and tongue."* (Revelation 7:9)

W<small>E SAW IN</small> C<small>HAPTER</small> 5 that the Second Vatican Council reminded us: "In celebrating the annual cycle of Christ's mysteries, holy Church honors with special love the Blessed Mary, Mother of God, who is joined by an inseparable bond to the saving work of her Son."[1]

When most Catholics think of devotion to Mary, they probably think of the rosary. The Church highly esteems the rosary and strongly recommends it, but Pope Paul VI cautioned that this "devotion should not be propagated in a way that is too one-sided or exclusive. The rosary is an excellent prayer, but the faithful should feel serenely free in this regard. They should be drawn to its calm recitation by its intrinsic appeal."[2] Pope Paul also made the point that the Church has a long history of Marian devotion, but she does not bind herself to any particular form of that devotion. The Church understands that

---

[1] *Constitution on the Sacred Liturgy*, no. 103.
[2] *Marialis Cultis*, no. 55.

certain outward religious expressions, while perfectly valid in themselves, may be less suitable to men and women of different ages and cultures.[3]

What is essential to authentic Marian devotion is full, active participation in the sacred liturgy during its official celebration of Marian feasts. The liturgy is an inexhaustible font of true Marian devotion. Of particular note are three solemnities: the Immaculate Conception on December 8, the Divine Motherhood on January 1, and the Assumption on August 15. Of course Mary is also the foremost person honored in the Solemnity of All Saints on November 1. In addition there is a long list of liturgical Marian days, some of which are Feasts, some Obligatory Memorials, and some Optional Memorials. On those Saturdays of Ordinary Time when no other feast or memorial is to be observed, the Church recommends that a Mass in honor of Mary be celebrated. There are approximately twenty such free Saturdays each year. Finally the name of Mary, Mother of God, is included in every eucharistic prayer without exception so that no Mass is celebrated without honor to Mary.

The arrangement of principal Marian feasts indicates an important fact about Mary. Her feasts parallel those of her son to manifest that she imitated Jesus; she lived his life. No human person planned this arrangement; it developed over the centuries under the guidance of the Holy Spirit. Notice the relationship of the feast days of Mary on the right to those of the Lord on the left:

Annunciation, March 25	Immaculate Conception, Dec. 8
Christmas, Dec. 25	Birth of Mary, September 8

---

[3] *Ibid.*, no. 36.

Presentation, Feb 2	Presentation Nov. 21
Passion	Seven Sorrows (Sept. 15)
Resurrection, Easter	Assumption, Aug. 15
Christ the King	Queenship of Mary, Aug. 22
Sacred Heart of Jesus	Immaculate Heart of Mary

All Catholics, no matter what their devotional tastes, should find in the sacred liturgy a full and beautiful expression of their devotion to the Blessed Virgin Mary, Mother of God and Disciple of Jesus.

All Saints and All Souls

When thinking about the saints, we begin with a consideration of two important days in the liturgical year, All Saints and All Souls. These two days emphasize the value of people in God's eyes. When Pope Pius XI instituted the feast of Christ the King in 1925, he placed it on the last Sunday of October so that it would be proximate to the feasts of All Saints and All Souls. He wanted to emphasize that people are the essential component of God's kingdom of holiness.[4]

In the New Testament era all living Christians were afforded the title of "saint." They were a "chosen race, a royal priesthood, a holy nation."[5] When persecutions raged against the Church, some Catholics were heroic by persevering in their faith despite threats, torture, and even death itself. The name of "saint" began to be reserved for martyrs who were conformed

---

[4] The reform of Vatican II moved the Solemnity of Christ the King to the final Sunday of the liturgical year in order to emphasize its eschatological character.

[5] 1 Peter 2:9.

to Christ in his death. But when persecutions ended, the Church broadened its vision of how people live the Christian life. It saw that dedicated Christians exemplify not only Christ's death but all aspects of his life: his love for his Father, his preaching, his intense prayer, his healing ministry to the sick, his love and concern for all classes of people, especially children and the poor.

Sanctity is conformity to Christ. Bishop Bossuet, remember, declared that the Church is Jesus Christ, extended in space and time and communicated to people. That could also be the description of sainthood. Christ is present and active in the world even after his ascension into heaven not only by means of the Eucharist, not only in the inspired word, but also in people. It is not merely that people are called to imitate Christ as a modern President of the United States might try to model himself on George Washington. Washington is dead. He cannot communicate anything of himself to one of his successors, but Jesus is alive and he certainly does communicate a share in his life to his people. Every person in union with Christ by baptism and faith continues Christ's presence in the world. Jesus lived the perfect human life, and his followers continue that life in varying degrees. Some people have lived the Christ-life to an eminent degree. We call them saints.

Since no one person can fully reflect the life of Christ, saints tend to specialize in certain aspects of the life of Christ by the manner in which they become conformed to the image of Christ. St. Francis of Assisi is the Christ who was so poor he had no place to lay his head. St. Teresa of Avila is the Christ who spent whole nights in prayer. St. Vincent de Paul is the Christ who was the evangelizer of the poor. St. Thérèse the Little Flower is the Christ who commanded us to become like little children and who lived the simplicity he commanded. The Curé of Ars is the Christ, the Lamb of God, who takes away the sins of the world.

For centuries the people of the Church gave the recognition of sainthood by acclamation. After the death of someone who seemed to have lived a life of intense union with Christ, the voice of the people declared that person to be a saint. Eventually an elaborate process, known as canonization, developed for determining who deserved official recognition as a person of extraordinary holiness. Now the Church is very careful that the person proposed for sainthood actually lived the Christ-life in what is called an heroic manner.

One unhappy effect of the canonization process is that it tends to scare us away from any serious thought of becoming a saint. We are not worthy of such aspirations, we protest. Sainthood is simply too much to hope for, we fear. You can even hear some people say, "I will be happy just to make it into purgatory." The Solemnity of All Saints helps to adjust our thinking. Although the great saints, Mary and Joseph, the apostles and martyrs, and all the "name" saints such as St. Anthony and Mother Cabrini, are included in the celebration, this is really a special day for the "little" saints, ordinary people like us who will never be formally canonized by the Church but who try to live according to God's will. Ordinary people are those who Jesus declares are mother, and brother, and sister to him.

Every saint shows us that saints are not self-made people. Sanctity is not something we achieve by our own ability. It is a gift which we accept from God. He is the one who makes people holy since, as we profess in the Third Eucharistic Prayer, all life, all holiness comes from God the Father. When we come to Mass we have before us the chief means for growth in holiness, the sacrament of the holy Eucharist. In giving us his body and blood Christ wants to draw us into communion with himself. Living in accord with our oneness with Christ leads us into God's kingdom of holiness.

Whatever may be our liturgical observance, music is an intrinsic part of the celebration. In Chapter 10 which follows we consider music and related elements.

Chapter 10

Liturgical Music

"Sing gratefully to God from your hearts in psalms, hymns, and inspired songs." (Colossians 3:16)

FROM THE BEGINNING OF CIVILIZATION music has been part of every culture. A strong instinct within human beings moves them to express their deepest emotions through song. The Church in the *Roman Missal* tells us that "song is the sign of the heart's joy," and St. Augustine said that "to sing belongs to lovers." He also added that "he who sings well, prays twice."[1] It is no wonder that the Holy Spirit through the apostle Paul encourages us to "sing gratefully to God from our hearts in psalms, hymns, and inspired songs."

The *Constitution on the Sacred Liturgy* of the Second Vatican Council devotes its sixth chapter to Sacred Music. This chapter is the primary source of principles which are intended to guide the use of music during liturgical celebrations, especially the Mass. The following is a free summary.

> The musical tradition of the Church is a treasure of greater value than that of any other art for the enhancement of liturgy. Music which is in accord with this tradition is intimately linked with the liturgical

---

[1] See the General Instruction of the *Roman Missal*, no. 19.

action, expresses prayerfulness, promotes solidarity and unity, and enriches the liturgical rites.

This tradition is not intended to exclude contemporary or cultural expressions. In fact, while diligently following liturgical directives, emphasis should be given to current and popular forms of devotional music. The organ has a long history in liturgical music, but other instruments are also to be used for the glory of God.

Contemporary composers are counseled to produce works of high quality, and they are not to confine themselves to those which only large choirs can sing, but are to provide for the needs of small choirs and for the active participation of the entire assembly. In fact, whenever the sacred action is to be celebrated with music, care must be exercised that the whole body of the faithful may be able to contribute that active participation which is rightly theirs.

Not all religious music is liturgical. It is such only when it is intimately linked with liturgical action, expresses prayerfulness, promotes solidarity and unity, and engages the participation of the people. [Mozart's "Requiem" is magnificently beautiful and inspirational religious music, but we do not attempt to sing it during a funeral Mass.]

Every aspect of liturgy, including music, is intended to help the people worship God in body as well as spirit, and to offer their voices as well as their hearts in union with the sacrificial action of Christ. Any Sunday Mass is incomplete unless it provides the people with the opportunity "to sing gratefully to God from their hearts." The fundamental directive for all aspects of liturgy, including music, is that expressed in the second chapter of the *Constitution on the Sacred Liturgy*: "The aim to be considered above all else is the full and active participation by all the people, for it is the primary and indispensable source from which the faithful are to derive the true Christian spirit."[2]

Who Does The Singing?

Before Vatican II singing at Mass in Latin was left to a choir or a soloist. Choirs must still be promoted, but their significant contribution to the excellence of the liturgy is not meant to exclude the faithful. In fact, the practice of assigning all the singing to the choir alone and excluding the people is forbidden. The choir and the people can participate together in several ways. The choir may sing a section of a composition, and the people repeat it. The choir and the people may alternate stanzas or verses of a hymn. What is often very effective is to have the choir add harmony to the melody which is sung by the people.

The choir may sing alone before the Mass begins, during the preparation of the gifts, and at the conclusion of Mass. No choir master or member should feel that the liturgy has minimized their role. Rather their dignity is truly that of Christ himself in that they are called to serve the people of God.

Official documents make no mention of a soloist other than that of the presiding priest whose solo voice, in spoken word or song, is the symbol that the people's prayer becomes one in Christ whose person the ordained priest represents and bears.

Soloists even when well intentioned rather often fall into the category of entertainment or at least call too much attention to themselves. A cantor is not a soloist but a singer who, in a sense, takes the place of the choir. The cantor intones and

---

[2] *Constitution on the Sacred Liturgy*, no. 14.

directs the singing of the people and may alternate parts with them in responsorial singing.

The Church excludes no type of sacred music from the Mass as long as it matches the character of the individual parts and helps the active participation of the people.

A Sunday Mass without singing does not satisfy the principle of full and active participation. It is like reflecting on the mysteries of the rosary without saying the "Hail Marys." It is fundamentally incomplete. The fact that singing is integral to the Mass does not mean that the entire Mass is to be sung, or that there is no preference for which parts should be put to music. Usually the easiest, but not the best, procedure is to sing four hymns: at the beginning, during the preparation of the gifts, during communion, and at the end of Mass. In some instances this amounts to singing within Mass but not singing the parts of the Mass which by their nature demand singing to express their full meaning. Acclamations are first in order of preference. These are the "Alleluia" which greets the gospel, the "Holy, holy, holy" which is part of the Preface, the Memorial Acclamation which proclaims the mystery of faith, the minor doxology after the Lord's Prayer which begins "For the kingdom, the power, and the glory are yours," and the Great Amen which concludes the eucharistic prayer.

It should be carefully noted that the Great Amen is not a response to the doxology which begins "Through him, with him, and in him." It is an expression of faith in response to the entire eucharistic prayer. For that reason this "Amen" should always be sung, even if the celebrant recites the doxology. The "Great Amen" may be repeated even several times for emphasis but the meaning of this word should not be obscured by the addition of other words which belong elsewhere, such as "Alleluia" or "forever and ever."

Ideally the responsorial psalm should be sung, usually with a cantor taking the verses of the psalm and the people taking the refrain. When all sing the "Our Father," its communitarian and joyful character is emphasized, but this prayer is not one which by its nature should be sung. Although priority should be given to singing the appropriate parts of the Mass, hymns which are suitable should not be excluded. In fact an entrance hymn ought not to be omitted. Purposes of the entrance hymn are to open the celebration, to deepen the unity of the people, to introduce the theme of the season or feast, and to accompany the procession These purposes guide the choice for the entrance hymn.

The people need not sing during the preparation of the gifts. There may be silence at this time or, outside of Advent and Lent, some form of instrumental music. The choir may sing alone. A hymn during the preparation of the gifts should not contain sentiments of offering as if our gifts were bread and wine and not the body and blood of Christ; rather this hymn may reflect the theme of the day or the season.

The communion song begins as soon as the priest receives the body of the Lord. It should emphasize and express the spiritual union of the communicants with Christ and through him with each other. All the people should join their voices in a single song which shows the joy of all and makes the communion procession an act of Christian community. Because the communion song is to begin as soon as the priest receives the body of the Lord, the choir or the cantor should go to communion last, not first, so as not to delay the beginning of this song. Since in some instances, maybe most, many people fail to join in the communion song, it is tempting for the choir or cantor simply to take over without any special effort to include the people. It is a serious mistake to give in to that temptation. It is very appropriate for the people to sing together during the moment when they deepen their union with Christ and through him with each other.

Singing is part of human celebration. I cannot imagine a group of people standing around a cake decorated with candles, and reciting to a friend or relative in a monotonous drawl the words, "Happy birthday to you, happy birthday to you...." When someone takes the lead and adds the traditional melody, these words come alive in a spirit of celebration. They unite the participants around the person who is observing his birthday.

Our celebration of birthdays, even with singing, lacks an important element. Little or no attention is usually paid to the parents. We should congratulate the birthday person, but parents deserve a salute of thanks. In the Mass Jesus, our priest and our leader, calls us together to celebrate our birth as God's children through his death and resurrection. God the Father, embracing his Son in his great act of love on the cross, reaches out to embrace us also as his sons and daughters. And so Jesus invites us, his sisters and brothers, to share in a salute of thanksgiving to our one heavenly Father. Jesus is the leader of our celebration, and he encourages us to join him in a song of celebration.

Perhaps it seems strange to think of Jesus as one who sings, and yet we should remember that the chief form of prayer for Jesus on this earth was the psalms. These inspired prayers, handed down from his ancestors, were composed to be sung. Devout Jews not only memorized these prayers but were familiar with traditional melodies which enhanced their meaning. Jesus and his disciples prayed the psalms, and it is quite likely that Jesus led their singing in a rich baritone. Saint Matthew in his account of the Last Supper indicates, "After singing songs of praise, they walked out to the Mount of Olives." As Jesus led the disciples in the ritual of the Last Supper, so he led them in its hymns.

At the Last Supper Jesus yearned and prayed for our unity: "Father, that they all may be one." At Mass music is a unifying force. In song we not only join in the same words but in the same melody. We give up our natural rhythms and melodies, peculiar to ourselves, in order to become one voice. This "sacrifice" is what makes singing difficult or objectionable for some people who protest that they "just don't like to sing."

Jesus our priest at Mass wishes us to join him in songs of praise to our heavenly Father. He is very pleased when unity is expressed through songs offered by all of us as the one voice of his mystical body.

Working against a spirit of full participation is the fact that movies and television have produced a climate of passivity among us. Many of us have become spectators rather than participants. In the world of music we are readily entertained by the performance of professionals, often to the detriment of singing or playing music ourselves.

Music is a magnificent gift from God and he wishes us to use it in lifting our hearts to him in worship. According to the principles of sound liturgy, music in worship should be a means of participation, not a form of entertainment. Music is not a performance to be admired, but a form of prayer to be shared and offered to God.

Taste varies greatly in music. This variety makes for disagreement about which kind of music is appropriate. What is ineffective or even distracting for one person may be truly devotional for another. Although it is often asserted that one cannot argue about taste, some general principles apply to liturgical music.

Good liturgical music is characterized by prayerfulness and simplicity. For music to be prayerful close attention must be given to the words so that they are in harmony with the spirit and the meaning of the liturgical action which they accompany. Simplicity means that the music is singable, which encourages participation. (Lest anyone think that the noble character of simplicity indicates inferior quality, he need only reflect on the Christmas hymn, "Silent Night," which could scarcely be more simple or more noble.)

There is a distinction between religious music and liturgical music. Religious music is based on themes of faith, as are some compositions by the classical masters. Liturgical music is that which is suitable for sharing by the priestly people of God as a form of their prayer. Excellence should be striven for in liturgical music, but God is more pleased by our sincerity than by our talent, and he is more glorified by our prayerful spirit and participation than he is by our artistic ability.[3]

In every instance we must remember that "the aim above all else is the full, active participation by all the people."

St. Paul wrote to the Ephesians: "Be filled with the Spirit, addressing one another in psalms and hymns and spiritual songs, singing and playing to the Lord in our hearts, giving thanks always and for everything in the name of our Lord Jesus Christ to God the Father."[4] Celebrating the Mass with song helps to achieve the ideal proposed in the Letter to the Romans that "according to the Spirit of Christ Jesus we may with one heart and one voice glorify God, the Father of our Lord Jesus Christ."[5]

---

[3] I have relied in this chapter on two official documents, *Musicam Sacram* which is a Vatican document and on *Music and Catholic Worship* which is a publication of the Bishops' Committee on the Liturgy. This brief chapter does not substitute for a study of these two documents.

[4] Ephesians 5:18-20.

[5] Romans 15:5-6.

Chapter 11

Art and Environment

*"He will show you an upstairs room, spacious, furnished,
and all in order. That is the place you are to get ready for us."*
(Mark 14:15)

A MAN WENT INTO A DARKENED theater, late for the movie. He
walked carefully down the aisle, looking for an empty seat.
When he spotted one, he genuflected in the aisle and took his
place. He felt as if he were in church. The one structure a Catholic church should not look like is a theater, and yet many of our
older churches were built in that style. In a theater the viewers
have no relationship with each other and their attention is fo-
cused on the screen in a passive or merely receptive manner.

A church is not a theater. Its purpose is to accommodate
the fourfold action of Christ during the celebration of the liturgy in the assembly, the priest, the word, and the Eucharist.[1]
The *Constitution on the Sacred Liturgy* states: "When churches
are to be built, let great care be taken that they be suitable for
the celebration of liturgical services and for the active participation of the faithful."[2]

---

[1]   Some of the material in this chapter is repeated from Chapter 6 in Volume Two
for convenience.

[2]   *Constitution on the Sacred Liturgy*, no. 124.

The place for the assembly is the first consideration and it is to be guided by the aim which is to be considered before all else, and that aim is to achieve full, active participation by all the faithful.[3] At liturgy people are participants, not spectators. The chief element of participation is the proper internal disposition, but that disposition is to be expressed externally. For that reason participation calls for the people "to take part by means of acclamation, responses, psalmody, antiphons, and songs, as well as by actions, gestures, and bodily attitudes."[4] Since the assembly forms "one body, one spirit in Christ," they are not to worship in isolation, as if in a theater where one sees only the back of the head of the person in front of him, but they are to be related to one another by being located, such as in a semi-circle around the altar, that they see and are aware of other persons. There should be no suggestion that the people are cut off from the sacred action so as to imply that what takes place at the altar is solely a clerical ritual in which they are to play merely a passive role. This separation would in effect deny the royal priesthood of the faithful and the teaching of Pope Pius XII that the people are to be "most closely united with the High Priest and his earthly minister at the time when the consecration of the divine Victim is effected and at that time especially when those solemn words are pronounced, 'Through him, with him, in him, in the unity of the Holy Spirit all glory and honor is yours, almighty Father, forever and ever.'"[5]

We commonly use the word "church" (with a lower case "c") to speak of the building in which people worship and the

---

[3] *Constitution on the Sacred Liturgy*, no. 14.
[4] *Ibid.*, no. 30.
[5] *Mediator Dei*, no. 109.

word "Church" (with an upper case "C") to mean the people themselves. In a much earlier era the building used for worship was called in Latin *Domus Ecclesiae,* the Home of the Church, that is, the home of God's people. We still speak of the church as the house of God, but God is our Father and so the church is our home and ought to appear as such.

The communion railing was, according to historians, introduced in England in order to keep the ruffians from disrupting the action at the altar. When people started to kneel for Holy Communion, the railing became a convenience for them, even though its origin had nothing to do with posture. Since the church should not appear to be a building of two rooms, one for the faithful and the other for the priest and ministers at the altar, there should no longer be a railing separating the people from the altar.

Equally the choir should not seem separate from the assembly, but it is very difficult to state firmly just where the choir should be located. In a choir loft? No, that clearly isolates the choir from the rest of the assembly. Behind the altar? No, that position seems to separate the choir from both altar and assembly.

To one side of the assembly area? Perhaps, but then in which direction do the choir members face, toward the altar or toward the rest of the assembly? It would seem that the director could be in a position which makes it possible to face both the choir and the people alternately, but I think I rather favor the choir members facing toward the altar. To face the people suggests to me that the choir is entertaining them. Maybe the distinct construction of each church building must determine the choir's location — in accord, however, with the guiding principle that the choir is part of the assembly.

The second consideration is the chair of the presider, the third is the ambo for the word, and the fourth is the altar for the Eucharist. I have discussed these three aspects of a church in Chapter 6 of Book 2.

It will surprise, perhaps even dismay, some Catholics to learn that the tabernacle is not one of the focal points of the liturgy nor is it even integral to the structure of a church building. Of course in the early Church the Eucharist was reserved only for the sake of communion to the sick. Over time, quite a few centuries in fact, there developed a devotion to the Real Presence of Christ so that a permanent place of repose for the Blessed Sacrament resulted, the tabernacle. In the minds of many the tabernacle, not the altar, seemed to be the center of a Catholic church. The teachings of the Second Vatican Council have returned us to the doctrine that the Eucharist is to be celebrated as the living memorial of the death and resurrection of Jesus. This does not mean that devotion to the Real Presence is to be abandoned, but it does mean that it must be put into proper perspective. In fact, following liturgical directives fosters, rather than suppresses, devotion to the Real Presence.

The General Instruction of the *Roman Missal* gives a directive which expresses the ideal to be striven for: "It is highly recommended (*valde commendandum est*) that the holy Eucharist be reserved in a chapel suitable for private adoration and prayer."[6] Implementation of this paragraph will satisfy the need for a quiet, devotional place for eucharistic reservation.

There should be provision for two moods or mentalities, one in the church for liturgical celebration which is ecclesial and

---

[6]   General Instruction of the *Roman Missal,* no. 276.

communal, and the other in a chapel for adoration which is private and personal. People should not have to adjust within the same space from one mentality and mood to the other. Experience proves that such adjustment is unworkable and often makes for hard feelings among the participants when one group wishes to act communally and another wishes to act privately.

There is a second, and somewhat more compelling, reason for a "Blessed Sacrament chapel." The *Instruction on the Worship of the Eucharistic Mystery* dated May 25, 1967, states "In the celebration of Mass the principal modes of worship by which Christ is present to his Church are gradually revealed. First of all, Christ is seen to be present among the faithful gathered in his name; then in his word, as the scriptures are read and explained; in the person of the minister; finally and in a unique way under the species of the Eucharist. Consequently, by reason of the symbolism, it is more in keeping with the nature of the celebration of the eucharistic presence of Christ, which is the fruit of the consecration and should be seen as such, should not be on the altar from the very beginning of Mass through the reservation of the sacred species in the tabernacle."[7] The *Ceremoniale Episcoporum* also directs that if the Blessed Sacrament is reserved in a tabernacle on the altar, it is to be transferred to a fitting place before the celebration of Mass.[8]

The Blessed Sacrament chapel should not be used for weekday Mass. The reasons are these: first, there is to be but one altar within the entire church, including the Blessed Sacrament chapel; secondly, as we have seen "by reason of the sym-

---

[7] *Instruction on the Worship of the Eucharistic Mystery*, II, D.

[8] *Ceremoniale Episcoporum*, no. 49.

bolism, it is more in keeping with the nature of the celebration of the eucharistic presence of Christ, which is the fruit of the consecration and should be seen as such, should not be on the altar from the very beginning of Mass through the reservation of the sacred species in the tabernacle"; and thirdly, the chapel is reserved for private devotion and not for liturgy.

The Church is bound in conscience to emphasize and exemplify the essential meaning of the Eucharist as it was instituted by Christ, while not neglecting a development of doctrine regarding the lasting presence of Christ after the liturgical celebration.[9]

The Baptismal Font

Churches which are yet to be built should have a baptistery, a room which is reserved for the sacrament of baptism. It should be large enough to accommodate not only a font but also a place for the Liturgy of the Word and for an assembly of the faithful. The room may be located in a chapel either inside or outside the church, or in some other part of the church easily seen by the faithful. It is also the area where the Easter candle is given a place of honor outside the Easter season (during the Easter season, it is to be in the body of the church) and where the holy oils may be displayed. If a separate room is not con-

---

[9]   History shows, especially during the development in the thirteenth century which we to a large extent have inherited, that people have rarely failed to accept the *res* of the *res et sacramentum* of the Eucharist, but they have frequently failed to understand and act in accord with the *sacramentum* of the *res et sacramentum*. Even today not enough Catholics manifest a proper understanding of the eucharistic celebration.

structed in the remodeling of older churches, there should be a space provided for baptism. Some liturgists insist that it is best placed at the main entrance of the church to symbolize that baptism is the *janua ecclesiae*, the door of the church, but others prefer that it be placed where the assembly can readily see the action of baptism, that is, near the front of the church. The rite of immersion is more suitable as a symbol of participation in the paschal mystery of the death and resurrection of Jesus, but the rite of infusion may lawfully be used in the celebration of baptism.[10]

The Penitential or Reconciliation Chapel

Most churches by now have provided some private space for "face-to-face" confession. In 1974 the National Conference of U.S. Bishops stated: "It is desirable that small chapels or rooms of reconciliation be provided in which penitents may choose to confess their sins through an informal face-to-face exchange with the priest... but it is also desirable that such rooms afford the option of the penitent's kneeling at the fixed confessional grill...."[11] The Bishops' Committee on the Liturgy added further that such rooms should be simple "with nothing in evidence beyond a simple cross, a table, and a Bible.... The word 'chapel' appropriately describes this space."[12]

---

[10] *Christian Initiation, General Introduction*, nos. 22-25.
[11] *Bishops' Committee on the Liturgy Newsletter* for Dec. 1974, no. 450.
[12] *Environment and Art in Catholic Worship*, no. 81.

Statues and Pictures

Concerning statues and pictures in churches the *Constitution on the Sacred Liturgy* is emphatic in principle and temperate in application: "The practice of placing sacred images in churches so that they may be venerated by the faithful is to be firmly maintained; nevertheless, their number should be moderate and their relative location should reflect right order. Otherwise they may create confusion among the Christian people and promote a faulty sense of devotion."[13] Ordinarily there should be only one image of each saint, but I know from experience, especially in Southern California, that sometimes this principle cannot be followed. In most churches of my area if there is a statue or picture of Our Lady of the Miraculous Medal, there must also be one of Our Lady of Guadalupe.

If there is a prominent cross or crucifix near the altar, the processional cross should be brought to the sacristy. Every church ought to have stations of the cross, which reflect the oldest of Catholic devotions.

Just as a church is not a theater, so it is not a showplace or museum for art, even sacred art; rather it should be a structure of noble beauty rather than mere extravagance.[14] The General Instruction of the *Roman Missal* states that art "is to aid faith and devotion and to be true to the reality which it is intended to symbolize and the purpose which it is to serve."[15]

A not uncommon opinion is that color is to be used to heighten the warmth of a church, to provide a pleasant atmo-

---

[13] *Constitution on the Sacred Liturgy*, no. 125.

[14] *Ibid.*, no. 124.

[15] General Instruction of the *Roman Missal*, no. 254.

sphere, and to reflect the liturgical season. In particular effort should be put forth to make good use of banners of color in accord with the liturgical season: white for Easter, white or gold for Christmas, violet for Lent and Advent, and green for ordinary time. Pentecost is a Sunday within the Easter season, in fact the final Sunday of the Easter season, but its color is red. Banners should derive their expressiveness from the elegance of their material and the richness of their color. Since color itself is a symbol, banners should ordinarily not be encumbered with other symbols, nor should they serve as places for slogans which detract from both their beauty and their meaning.

Although the celebration of the Eucharist is the primary action within a church, planning or renovation should take into account the richness of Catholic worship. Just as the liturgy encompasses more than the Mass, so the church building should be a suitable place for all the sacraments, for a celebration of the Liturgy of the Hours, and for devotions such as the public making of the stations and the recitation of the rosary.

Church buildings, although all serving the same purpose, are not to be identical since we are a Catholic, a universal Church. What is attractive in Holland is not appealing in Honduras. Our Catholicity creates a tension between the appropriateness of reflecting that which is particular to a culture or locale and the necessity of revealing the universal character of our religion. The document, *Environment and Art in Catholic Worship*, states: "Although the art and decoration of the liturgical space is to be that of the local culture, identifying symbols of particular cultures, groups, or nations are not appropriate as permanent parts of the liturgical environment. While such symbols might be used for a particular occasion of holiday, they should not regularly constitute a part of the environment of common prayer."[16]

Some Official Sources

Some official, although scanty, sources are available for art and environment which are second only to music as controversial aspects of liturgy. The first is the *Constitution on the Sacred Liturgy* by the Second Vatican Council, Chapter VII: "Sacred Art And Sacred Furnishing" (only three pages in length). The second is the General Instruction of the *Roman Missal*, Chapter V: "Arrangement and Furnishing of Churches for the Eucharistic Celebration," together with the Appendix for the Dioceses of the United States (only slightly more ample than the material in the *Constitution on the Sacred Liturgy*). Both are found in the front of the Sacramentary. The third is *Instruction of the Congregation of Rites for the Proper Implementation of the Constitution on the Sacred Liturgy*, Chapter 6. The fourth is *Environment and Art in Catholic Worship* by the Bishops' Committee on the Liturgy (54 pages) which is due for a revision.[17]

---

[16] *Environment and Art in Catholic Worship*, no. 101.

[17] For a reason I have not been able to understand at least one prelate in the United States vehemently condemns this document as lacking in any authority. Actually it was published on November 2, 1977 by the Bishops' Committee on the Liturgy with a Foreword by Archbishop John Quinn, then Chairman of the Bishops' Committee on the Liturgy. That looks like pretty good authority to me. The content is far from radical or extreme although I must admit that the pictures in the back will never win a contest.

Chapter 12

Vestments, Robes, and Sunday Best

"They stood before the throne of the Lamb,
dressed in long white robes..." (Revelation 7:9)

AMONG ALL THE PRESSING NEEDS which face us in the liturgy, it
may seem trivial to consider what people should wear for the
celebration of Sunday Eucharist. Actually the topic reaches into
important principles upon which decisions should be based.

The Second Vatican Council teaches that "the liturgy is
the outstanding means by which the faithful can express in their
lives and manifest to others the mystery of Christ and the real
nature of the true Church."[1] Ecclesiology and liturgy affect each
other. Before Vatican II we experienced a liturgy which expressed an ecclesiology that had developed from the post-ref-
ormation era. At that time the Magisterium found it necessary
to emphasize, among other matters, the centrality of hierarchi-
cal authority and the necessity of ordained ministers for liturgical rites. This ecclesiology was reflected in the missal of Pius V
and continued with only modest variations by Pius XII and John
XXIII until Paul VI promulgated his missal in 1969. The lit-

---

[1] *Constitution on the Sacred Liturgy*, no. 2.

urgy had become clericalized; there seemed to be little need for full, active participation by the people not only in the liturgy, but in the Church which was reflected in the liturgy. As a consequence, Pope Pius XI could describe Catholic action as the participation of the laity in the apostolate of the hierarchy. The Second Vatican Council did more than turn the altar around. It turned the definition of Catholic action around because it taught that the Church means people and that Christ is present and active at liturgy in the first instance within the assembly. In accord with this renewed ecclesiology, Pope John Paul II at his General Audience on July 20, 1991 described the Church as the messianic assembly of God's People. We become part of this people, God's family here on earth, through the sacraments of Christian initiation.

People need to consider two things when they are deciding what to wear to church on Sunday. The first is their own dignity. Through baptism they have become "a chosen race, a royal priesthood, a holy nation, a people God claims for his own."[2] I doubt that anyone would be satisfied to see the presider at Mass attired in a tank top and shorts. It would be beneath his dignity. But the dignity of the ministerial priest derives from the fact that Christ has chosen him from among the people of the royal priesthood. Ministerial priesthood serves the royal priesthood. Surely, then, those who are of the royal priesthood should be suitably attired.

The second thing to be considered is the involvement of the people in the celebration of the Eucharist. The ecclesiology of Vatican II manifests that baptism is not a passive power, as

---

[2]   1 Peter 2:9f.

some theologians taught before the Council, but an active one. The People of God are called to worship him in spirit and in truth. That is one reason why the *Constitution on the Sacred Liturgy* declares that the aim above all else in liturgical renewal is the full, active participation by the people. The sacredness of the eucharistic celebration urges that all participants should, by their dress, manifest the importance of what they are doing.

In scripture clothing is an external symbol of an internal reality. It should be such in liturgy too. St. Paul wrote to the Galatians to remind them that "those who have been baptized into Christ Jesus have clothed themselves with him" (3:27). Since all the baptized have been clothed in Christ, everyone in the assembly should manifest through their attire "the dignity of the royal priesthood." Some people object that they want to be as relaxed in church as at home, and they observe that since God is our Father the church is their home. The observation is correct, but we must remember that our Father is a King and all his children are royalty. Because of our baptism there is for us a spiritual *noblesse oblige*: we owe it to God and each other to act in accord with our dignity.

White is the color of baptism (that is why the alb, a white garment, is the vestment common to all liturgical ministers). In many parishes parishioners respond each year to the invitation to wear something white for the celebration of Easter. The effect is impressive (but not quite as impressive as when on Pentecost Sunday they wear something red). What is to be done on other Sundays? People should be encouraged to wear the best they have. "Sunday best" used to be a norm for going to church. Sunday Mass is not something people "catch" on their way to the beach or to a movie. Sunday Mass is the means by which

Catholics are to show forth the mystery of Christ and the real nature of the true Church. Liturgy is incarnational. It expresses inner reality through external signs which should not be minimalized. Not to be neglected is the best way to manifest the truth that through baptism we have been clothed in Christ Jesus.

In this matter we must be careful not to judge others. St. James in his Epistle reminds us not to show favoritism to the affluent person who is fashionably dressed over the poor person who appears in shabby clothes.[3] And yet even those with a scanty wardrobe and meager financial resources find something suitable to wear to a wedding. The Eucharist is "the wedding feast of the Lamb."[4]

Some parishes have abandoned the alb for lay ministers because they fear that people see it as a clerical garment. They say that the ministers should be attired in lay clothing, but they are actually referring to secular clothing. We must reclaim the word "lay" from professional people who misuse it. By the word "lay" they mean the uninitiated. But "lay" signifies just the opposite. It refers to the initiated, those people who have been incorporated into the Church through the sacraments of Christian initiation. The alb is the sign of this reality. We should be at pains to explain the symbolism of the alb, the white robe, to insist that it is a lay garment, the sign that "those who have been baptized into Christ Jesus have clothed themselves with him."[5] Particularly incongruous, however, is the situation in which some ministers wear albs, or the surplice as a substitute, and

---

[3]   James 2:1ff.
[4]   Revelation 19:9.
[5]   Galatians 3:27.

others do not. Altar servers should not be the only ministers other than the presider to be properly robed. Nor should readers wear secular dress when eucharistic ministers are attired in albs. Most improper of all, in my judgment, is that the presider alone wears an alb with his chasuble; that makes him appear to be unique, completely unlike any other minister, and improperly segregated from the community. A need for proper symbolism urges us to follow the directive which states that the alb is the garment which is common to all ministers.[6] In many parishes this directive has been implemented with happy results. The albs are of both masculine and feminine design, and their use not only provides a liturgical symbolism but also obviates the problem of both ostentation and impropriety in dress by the ministers. Presenting a brief instruction to the assembly periodically on these matters is very helpful.

Related to the principle concerning proper attire is the directive of the General Instruction which states that "the priest and ministers have their place in the part of the church which brings out their distinctive role, namely, to preside over the prayers, to proclaim the word of God, or to minister at the altar."[7] In some parishes the ministers sit in the pews and come and go, to and from the ambo or the altar, brought up from the assembly as if they were simply *ad hoc* helpers rather than liturgical ministers. The reason for this strange maneuver, some say, is that the ministers should appear as part of the assembly. Of course they are part of the assembly, but so is the presider. We must avoid suggesting that the presider is the sole, or only

---

[6] General Instruction of the *Roman Missal*, no. 298.

[7] *Ibid.*, no. 257.

really important, liturgical minister, or that he is not part of the worshiping community. All the ministers, including the presider, should appear as members of the community, the family, but ministers who are privileged to serve the family in a special way are given a symbolic place. All are equal in the Church but not all are the same. The Church is not really a unity; it is a harmony of many parts which come together through the power of the Holy Spirit to form the Body of Christ. Liturgy is to manifest this harmony. Those serving the Mass, by which I mean the priest and all the ministers, are not representatives of the community. No representation is needed since the community is present. Rather those serving should be a *mirror* of the community, a liturgical sign of the local Church. Those who minister within the liturgy need not be the same persons as those who minister outside the liturgy, but liturgical ministry is a sign that the parish is a community of service. It might be considered that if a parish has no lay ministers for service outside the liturgy, lay ministers within the liturgy are a contradiction.

In a movie or a play actors put on costumes in order to impersonate the characters whom they represent. The characters, of course, are not their actual identity. Just the opposite is true during the celebration of liturgy. Vestments are not costumes. They do not conceal the true identity of those wear them; they reveal it.

The fundamental vestment is the alb. It is also the first vestment in time since, even before the presider wore vestments, the newly baptized were clothed in a white garment, an alb. The white garment of baptism is symbolic of "putting on Christ," of entering into a relationship of oneness with Christ and all the people of his Church. Baptism makes us "a royal priesthood," and it is through this first of all the sacraments that we have the right and the power to participate in the liturgy.

When you see the ministers so robed, you may well think of the question posed in the Book of Revelation: "Who are these people all dressed in white?" The answer is: "These are the ones who have washed their robes and made them white in the blood of the Lamb" (7:14). Seeing the alb should remind all the people of the assembly of their own baptism and the privilege and power to participate in the celebration of the sacred liturgy.

Although we speak of "white people," that designation is quite inaccurate. No member of the human race is actually white, not even albinos. We are all of varied hues. The white alb represents Christ, the Head of the Church, in union with all of his members. That symbolism is derived from the fact that the color white is made up of all the visible rays of the spectrum. No one person is white, but all of us conjoined with Christ are white.

In the earliest eras of the Church, no specific vestments were worn other than the alb until perhaps the beginning of the fifth century. Everyone, including the priest, wore "Sunday best." Vestments were developed not only for the sake of decorum but for symbolic reasons. Over his baptismal alb a priest wears a stole, a strip of material which hangs from around his neck down to his knees. (Deacons wear a stole over their left shoulder to distinguish them from priests.) The stole is probably derived from the fact that ancient Roman officials wore a kind of scarf as a sign of authority. The stole may be used by the priest outside of Mass for the celebration of the other sacraments and the Liturgy of the Hours. At Mass a priest wears also a chasuble, the outer garment which is the sign of the joyful celebration of the holy Eucharist. (Nothing, including the stole, should ever obscure the importance of the chasuble by being placed over it.) The chasuble worn over the stole and the alb is a sign that the priest, baptized as a Catholic, has been given another sacrament, that of ordination, so that he may serve God's holy people most characteristically in the celebration of the holy Eucharist. The word "chasuble" is derived from the Latin, *casula,* which means "little house" (note the similarity with the Spanish *casa).* The chasuble should remind us that we come to church as to the house of God for the family celebration of our salvation in Christ. Vestments at Mass are important symbols of the identity of priest and people.

Chapter 13

Posture and Gestures

"Get up now and stand on your feet." (Acts 26:16)

CATHOLIC LITURGY IS INCARNATIONAL in the sense that the body as well as the soul, the material as well as the spiritual, are an expression of worship. We belong to God in all aspects of our humanity, and so we owe God worship by means of all aspects of our humanity, including posture and gestures.

The revised English language missal contains guidelines which are known as "pastoral introductions." The following is an excerpt from the section on posture: "Most English-speaking cultures share a common understanding of the significance of standing, sitting, and kneeling. One rises to greet people, to honor someone important, to express readiness for actions or when seized with excitement. In Christian liturgical tradition, standing is the basic posture of an Easter people lifted up to greet their risen Lord. One kneels as a human gesture of submission. In Christian tradition kneeling is an acknowledgment of creatureliness before God. It can signify penitence for sin, humility, reverence, and adoration."

The document, *Environment and Art in Catholic Worship,* says much the same regarding posture: "...sitting for preparations, for listening, and for silent reflection; standing for the gospel, solemn prayer, and praise and acclamation; kneeling for adoration and penitential rites."[1]

The pastoral introduction also indicates that "the Conference of Bishops may determine when the assembly should stand, sit, or kneel at Mass in accord with local sensibilities and the character of the rite." The two, sensibilities and the character of the rite, must be in harmony. When the sensibilities of the people are not in accord with the character of the rite, instruction is called for. Actually the first rule for posture is "For the sake of uniformity in movement and posture, the people should follow the directions given during the celebration by the deacon, the priest, or another minister."[2] Deviation from the posture of the assembly in protest is quite inappropriate and disturbing.

At Mass all rise to begin the entrance song. During the penitential rite, especially during Lent, it is appropriate to kneel and then to rise for the Opening Prayer. All sit during the readings in an attitude of attentiveness. All rise to greet the gospel, or more precisely to greet Christ who will speak to us in the gospel, and remain standing out of reverence during its proclamation. All sit to listen to the homily and stand for the Profession of Faith and the Prayer of the Faithful. All sit during the Preparation of the Gifts and stand for the Prayer Over the Gifts.

The Eucharistic Prayer

What of posture during the eucharistic prayer? This question necessitates a somewhat lengthy treatment. The presider

---

[1]   *Environment and Art in Catholic Worship*, no. 57.

[2]   General Instruction of the *Roman Missal*, no. 21.

and concelebrants stand throughout the prayer; no one seems to have a problem with that. Controversy swells around the posture of everyone else. The General Instruction of the *Roman Missal* states: "Unless provision is made otherwise at every Mass the people should stand... from the Prayer Over the Gifts to the end of Mass...." That directive obviously includes the eucharistic prayer but it goes on to say, "They (the people) should kneel at the consecration unless prevented by the lack of space, the number of the people, or some other good reason."[3] In November of 1969 the U.S. Conference of Bishops decreed that "the General Instruction should be adapted so that the people kneel beginning after the singing or recitation of the Sanctus until after the Amen of the eucharistic prayer, that is, before the Lord's Prayer."[4] The Bishops were within their rights when they adapted the directive of the missal but the missal clearly states that "adaptations must correspond to the meaning and character of each part of the celebration."[5] Quite honestly it is difficult, if not impossible, to see that the adaptation by the U.S. Conference of Bishops is in accord with the meaning and character of the eucharistic prayer.

To begin with, all of the Eucharistic Prayers refer to the assembly as standing during the Eucharistic Prayer. The Second Prayer says to the Father: "We thank you for counting us worthy to stand in your presence and serve you."[6] The First Eucharistic Prayer, the Roman Canon, says, "Remember all of us gath-

---

[3] *Ibid.*

[4] See the Appendix to the General Instruction of the *Roman Missal* for the Dioceses of the United States of America, no. 21.

[5] General Instruction of the *Roman Missal*, no. 21.

[6] Some priests, seeing the people kneeling, say in place of the prescribed translation, "We thank you for counting us worthy to be in your presence and serve you."

ered here before you," but the Latin says, "*Mememto... omnium circumstantium...,"* which means "Remember... all those standing around." People stood around the altar to form a *corona*, a crown. Inexplicably, "*circumstantium*" has been translated as "gathered here before you." The Third Eucharistic Prayer refers to the people as those whom God has willed to stand before him, the Latin being "...*quam tibi astare voluisti.*" Even though it is God's will that his people stand before him, the translators have seen fit to render this important truth as "the family you have gathered here before you." The Fourth Eucharistic Prayer uses the same term as does the First Prayer, "*circumstantium,*" which somehow was turned into the sterile phrase, "those here present." Except in the Second Eucharistic Prayer ("We thank you for counting us worthy to stand in your presence and serve you"), our translators have prevented us from perceiving the strong precedent and preference for standing during the eucharistic prayer.[7] What is true of these four Eucharistic Prayers is true of all the Eucharistic Prayers in current use.

It is a strange deviation at this stage of liturgical development to continue with an exception to the General Instruction. The new Sacramentary will provide a suitable occasion for a restoration of the original directive. Even now it is difficult to understand why a diocesan bishop does not have the right to invoke the General Instruction of the *Roman Missal* in his own diocese, especially in a matter which is a directive and not a constitutive law.

---

[7]   Although it is possible in Latin to use the verb, *stare*, to stand, as a copulative verb without reference to bodily deportment (e.g., *in medio stat virtus*, "virtue stands in the middle"), both history and the context of the Sacramentary confirm that in the eucharistic prayers "standing" describes the posture of the participants.

In many places outside the United States the practice among the people is to stand throughout the eucharistic prayer, except that in some instances they kneel at the Epiclesis and rise after the Consecration. More commonly they simply stand throughout the entire prayer. Actually the Latin verb which is translated as "kneel" is *"genuflectant,"* which literally means to bend the knee, to genuflect. Strictly speaking, the people could obey the rubrics by genuflecting together with the priest after the showing of the host and the chalice respectively. Perhaps it would be more fitting for the people to do what concelebrants do, which is to bow after the consecration.

Standing at the Foot of the Cross

During the eucharistic prayer we are privileged to do what Mary did on Calvary. St. John, who is very precise in his use of words, tells us that Mary *stood* at the foot of the cross.[8] When St. John wished to indicate merely that Mary was present at the marriage feast of Cana, he used a form of the verb "to be." The verb he used for Mary's posture at the cross means, not merely to stand, but to stand upright. Mary was joined by her sister, Mary the wife of Clopas, Mary Magdalene, and the beloved disciple. In the words of Pope Pius XII, "United with her Son, Mary offered him on Calvary to the Eternal Father."[9] It can be our great privilege to join Mary, to stand with her during the eucharistic prayer in order to do what she did at the cross. We are urged to unite with Mary's Son through the priest who bears

---

[8] John 19:25.
[9] *Mystici Corporis*, no. 127.

the person of Christ who offers the sacrifice in the name of all his members.

Standing for Sacrifice

Some Catholics think, for various reasons, that there is not enough emphasis on the Mass as sacrifice. They may not realize that kneeling during the eucharistic prayer suggests adoring Christ in the Eucharist rather than joining with him in the sacrifice which he offers to the Father. Adoring Christ is not the same as joining him in his offering of sacrifice. It is not right to maintain that kneeling enhances belief in the real presence and that standing diminishes it, just as it is not right to say that those who kneel for communion deny the resurrection. (Standing is the ancient as well as the contemporary posture for professing the resurrection.) Actually kneeling deflects the attention of the people away from the true character of the eucharistic prayer, especially the consecration. Pope Pius XII in 1947 insisted that the people offer the Mass in union with Christ and are "to be most closely united to the High Priest and his earthly minister at the time the consecration of the divine victim is effected." At Mass Christ is our mediator with the Father, our intercessor, our priest. It is essential that we look with him to the Father, and that we join him in the reality of the offering of his one sacrifice. Standing is the posture for offering.

Standing in order to offer the sacrifice with Christ, rather than kneeling to adore him, reflects our doctrine of the Blessed Trinity. The Eucharist is offered to the Father through Christ his Son in the unity of the Holy Spirit. This Trinitarian orientation, which is indispensable to the true Christian spirit, is expressed mightily in the conclusion of every eucharistic prayer: "Through him, with him, in him, in the unity of the Holy Spirit, all glory and honor is yours, almighty Father, forever and ever." This conclusion summarizes the meaning of the entire eucharistic prayer, including the consecration.

Priest and people act together during the eucharistic prayer. To be precise, "the priest at the altar bears the person of Christ who offers the sacrifice in the name of all his members."[10] But when the priest stands and the people kneel during the prayer it seems that priest and people are doing different things. People who are kneeling appear distanced from the priest. In fact, the only time now that the people kneel while the priest stands to pray in their name is during part of the eucharistic prayer. For all other prayers priest and people stand together. That is the way it should be during the eucharistic prayer.

The Communion Rite

Standing is the prescribed posture during the communion rite, although this prescription is unevenly observed in the United States.[11] The communion rite should be seen as fulfilling the words of Jesus during the consecration in the eucharistic prayer: "Take and eat... this is my body. Take and drink... this is the cup of my blood." Standing during both the eucharistic

---

[10] *Mediator Dei*, no. 93.

[11] General Instruction of the *Roman Missal*, no. 21: the people are to stand from the Prayer over the Gifts to the end of Mass, but they may sit, if this seems helpful, during the period of silence after communion.

prayer as well as during the communion rite indicates the harmonious relationship between the two.

A question which needs to be answered is why everyone seems to find it appropriate to stand while offering to the Father the prayer which Jesus taught us, the Lord's Prayer, and yet some find it suitable to kneel while offering to the Father the sacrifice which Jesus instituted. Actually the Lord's Prayer has acquired remarkable prominence. Not only do people stand throughout the "Our Father" and either say or sing it together, in many instances they have been advised to join hands during it, some going to great length across an aisle to reach out to a neighbor. The fact is that, important and traditional though the "Our Father" is, it is not essential as is the eucharistic prayer. The eucharistic prayer must not appear to be a prayer which is offered by the priest alone, while the people, with no apparent relationship with each other, kneel passively behind pews which suggests a separation from what is transpiring at the altar in the person of Christ who offers the sacrifice in the name of all his members. The priest is obliged to stand during the eucharistic prayer. His posture has never been interpreted as lacking in reverence or propriety. It is appropriate for both priest and people to stand throughout the eucharistic prayer. Kneeling is not more reverent than standing during the eucharistic prayers just as taking communion on the tongue is not more reverent that taking communion in the hand.

Some Difficulties

Some people may find it difficult to stand throughout the eucharistic prayer either because they are not well or because they find standing too tiring. Such persons should not hesitate to be seated. Actually some of us older people find kneeling difficult because of arthritic knees or other problems, and standing is welcomed. Standing will eliminate the three point posture (two knees on the kneeler and the backside against the pew) which is neither dignified nor appropriate.

It is customary to stand during the proclamation of the passion, which takes almost four times longer than any eucharistic prayer. Most people manage to stand throughout the passion, and those who cannot should be invited to be seated. The same course can be followed regarding the eucharistic prayer.

A Proper Perspective

Of course Christ in the Eucharist is divine and worthy of adoration, but that act of adoration should be fostered outside of Mass. Priests should encourage people to visit the Blessed Sacrament and should supply appropriate devotions, such as benediction. And yet with correct understanding we should see that proper participation in the Mass does not neglect an awareness of and appreciation for the real presence. Standing is not only the posture of those who offer the sacrifice with Christ to the Father; it is also a sign of reverence and attention. We should not think that the only way to show reverence for the real presence of Christ in the Eucharist is to kneel. We stand for the gospel out of reverence for the sacred words because the Church teaches us that "it is Christ himself who speaks to us when the holy scriptures are read in the church" (*Constitution on the Sacred Liturgy*, no. 7). We stand to proclaim the words of the Creed which express our faith. Equally it is appropriate to stand out of reverence for the gospel words of Christ during the consecration and for the reality of his presence and action in the holy Eucharist, the heartbeat of our faith. It is kneeling during the eucharistic prayer that is the anomaly, not standing. The question is not, "Why should we stand during the eucharistic prayer?", but "Why is anyone kneeling?"

Liturgical Gestures

Human hands are beautiful and expressive. How we use them is a part of our worship. I have not discovered to my satisfaction the origin of placing the palms of our hands against each other, fingers held straight and the right thumb crossed over the left. Nowhere in either the Old or the New Testament is there anything to suggest that this gesture is one of prayer. Some liturgists say that this practice originated in medieval Europe. To show his allegiance a knight knelt before his lord, joined his hands and placed them in the lap of his lord who in turn grasped the knight's hands in his own.[12] The Sacramentary now recommends the *orans* gesture (the plural seems better, *orantes*), which is described as arms forward and palms facing upward toward heaven. The First Letter to Timothy seems to suggest something like that: "It is my wish that in every place the men should pray, lifting up holy hands...."[13] Holding hands during the "Our Father" and of raising them toward heaven for the doxology which follows are "unofficial" actions. Actually there are no *prescribed*

---

[12] Actually there is a ceremony which fits this description during ordination when the ordinand promises obedience to his bishop.

[13] 1 Timothy 2:8.

gestures for the assembly. Local customs should prevail provided they are in accord with the nature of the rite.

The presider at times is told to join his hands and at other times to extend them, but with no description of what that means. For example the Sacramentary indicates that "with hands joined" he says, "Let us pray," and then he "extends his hands" to say the prayer. The gesture of the presider should suggest that he is gathering the prayers of the assembly and offering them to God.

Three priests were debating the appropriate posture for prayer. The first insisted that kneeling was the most proper since kneeling, he said, expresses our humility and reverence. The second preferred standing since, he said, standing is the traditional manifestation of our faith in the resurrection. The third said, "I did my best praying on the flat of my back as they were wheeling me into the operating room for by-pass surgery."

Whether we stand, sit, or kneel, we should recognize that posture is part of our worship of God.

Chapter 14

Culture and Liturgy

"I begin to see how true it is that God shows no partiality, that the people of any nation who fear God and act uprightly are acceptable to him." (Acts 10:34-35)

LET'S GO BACK TO THE YEAR 1944. We are making a movie about Catholics. We call it "Going My Way." The star is Bing Crosby who plays the part of a young priest whose name is Father O'Malley. The role of his pastor is given to Barry Fitzgerald who, if he were any more Irish, would not be able "to-talk-a-tall." Father O'Malley, to show that he is "cool," at times wears a sweat shirt with "Notre Dame, the Fighting Irish," emblazoned on the front. In the rectory is a prominent picture of Pope Pius XII, who had been born Eugenio Pacelli. That was the image of the Church in the United States: Irish immigrants and their offspring who paid allegiance to an Italian pope. Even though the Irish were not the only Catholics, they had for various reasons risen to such an ascendancy, especially in the episcopacy, that they put their imprint on the American Church. (I mean no disrespect to the Irish; otherwise, Rosalie Flanagan, my maternal grandmother who is now in heaven, would be very upset with me.)

Let's move to 1994, only fifty years later. The young priest could be named Martinez or Nguyen or Kim or Ikeocha. His pastor might be Msgr. Moretti or Msgr. Chang or Msgr. Lapid. All looked to Rome where they saw, not an Italian, but a Polish Pope. The image of the Church in the United States had changed to include a large number of ethnic and cultural expressions, to be what the Church had to struggle to become from the day of Pentecost, to be more Catholic. In this chapter I will treat several aspects of the subject but only, I realize, inadequately. My intention is simply to lay down a foundation for further thought and study.

The Struggle To Be Catholic

After Jesus ascended into heaven, his disciples were alone and confused. They were not quite sure what they should do or even what it meant to be a disciple of Jesus. Were they another Jewish sect such as the Pharisees, or the Zealots, or the Essenes? They needed the Holy Spirit to enlighten them. On the day of Pentecost the apostles remembered Jesus' parting words to them: "You will receive power when the Holy Spirit comes upon you; then you are to be my witnesses in Jerusalem, throughout Judea and Samaria, yes, even to the ends of the earth." Things became clearer. They were to move beyond Jerusalem and Judea and Samaria into Gentile territory. The realization that Gentiles were called as well as Jews made them understand that Jesus had done something new. Antioch in Gentile Syria beyond the boundaries of Judea and Israel became the center for a large number of disciples, and it was in Antioch that the disciples were called Christians for the first time.[1]

---

[1] Acts 11:26.

Only after much discussion, debate, and at times very heated arguments did the Christians come to see that Jesus had founded a Church for all people of all times and all places. Then St. Ignatius, the bishop of Antioch, around the year 100 A.D. used the term "Catholic" for the first time to refer to his Christian community. The word, of course, means "universal." It is most appropriate for the Church of Jesus Christ, and the name eventually became permanent and official. We now express our belief in the "One, Holy, *Catholic*, and Apostolic Church."

The Church is not Italian or Irish or Polish. It is not Mexican or American or Canadian. It is universal. Pope Paul VI said of his predecessor, John XXIII, that "he personified and expressed an essential characteristic of the Catholic Church, namely its universality and internationalization."[2] The vision of John XXIII influenced the Second Vatican Council which was a striking witness to the Catholicity of the Church. When the First Vatican Council met in 1869 there were bishops from all over the world but they were not indigenous bishops. For the most part they were European, even those who came from the United States. At Vatican II the bishops were not only *from* all the countries of the world, they were *of* all the countries in the world.

When the *Constitution on the Sacred Liturgy* was published on Dec. 4, 1963 it soon became obvious that the goals which the *Constitution* nobly expressed could be achieved only by a return to the vernacular in liturgical celebrations. I say "return" because the original practice was to celebrate the liturgy in the language of the people. In fact, the reason that Latin became a

---

[2] Homily at Milan on June 7, 1963.

liturgical language in the first place was due to the principle that the language of the liturgy should be the language of the people. In Rome until the third century the liturgy was celebrated in Greek. It was probably Pope Callistus, a simple man who had at one time been a slave, who first insisted that Greek, despite its elegance and rich vocabulary, should be replaced by Latin since Latin had become the vernacular.

Under the influence of Rome, Latin became widespread but it was not at any time the liturgical language of the universal Church. The Eastern Churches in union with the Pope all employed their own languages up to and beyond the Second Vatican Council, not only in the countries of their origins but even in the United States.

Pope John Paul II gave excellent witness to the importance of the vernacular by celebrating Mass in the language of the people wherever he went, sometimes spending many hours in preparation with tutors in languages with which he was not familiar. It is reported that he had the most difficulty with Korean but he insisted on mastering enough of that language to celebrate Mass for the people of Korea in their own language. The vernacular is sometimes called the mother tongue. The Pope recognized that there can be no substitute for the language which we learned as children from our mothers.

When the liturgy employs the multiple languages of God's people, the experience of Pentecost is repeated. On the first Pentecost, even though the people were from diverse regions throughout the Near East, they all heard the apostles speaking in their own tongue about the marvels God had accomplished in his Son. The importance, then, of every vernacular must be insisted upon. That God is worshiped in the multiple languages of his diverse children reflects the catholicity of our faith. Pope

John Paul II declared in his book, *Crossing the Threshold of Hope*, that the Second Vatican Council was like a new Pentecost for the Church. In celebrating the liturgical observance of Pentecost we give thanks and praise to God for calling us into the Church which is One, Holy, Catholic, and Apostolic.

The change from Latin with its European roots to the vernaculars of the world was more than a way of facilitating full, active participation in the liturgy; it was an expression of a deeper understanding of the Church as Catholic. Latin, or any single language, is not the means for oneness in the Church. Sharing in the word of God and the same holy Eucharist is the means for the Church to be both one and holy. Actually Latin is well honored in her daughters, especially Italian, Spanish, and Portuguese, which have softened her pronunciation, simplified her grammar, and enriched her vocabulary. Not just these Romance languages but all the many vernaculars of the liturgy manifest that the Church has been true to its mission to make disciples of all the nations, and these languages are a sign that the Church is now truly Catholic or universal.

Guidelines for Multilingual Masses

Culture involves more than language and yet language is one of the chief expressions of culture. The Federation of Diocesan Liturgical Commissions in 1987 developed guidelines, and they are only guidelines and not directives, for multilingual Masses. The guidelines make a very important point by insisting that as a matter of policy parishes are to provide Masses to meet the language needs of their people, and that multilingual Masses are arranged only on special occasions to join people of two or more cultures and languages in a single celebration. The matter of multilingual and multicultural liturgies is not lacking in difficulties and disagreements, but those who prepare multicultural or multilingual liturgies should consult, and as far as possible, follow the guidelines of the FDLC.

The Church was multilingual from the beginning. As the Church was born from the pierced side of Christ when he hung upon the cross, above his head was the inscription, "Jesus of Nazareth, King of the Jews." It was written in Hebrew, Latin, and Greek, which were the languages, in addition to Aramaic, spoken in Palestine. Some scholars are of the opinion that Jesus knew something of all of these languages, but his vernacular was Aramaic. The Old Testament was composed in Hebrew, except for the deutero-canonical books which were in Greek. Some say that the original of St. Matthew's gospel was Hebrew, but a better opinion seems to be that it was Aramaic. Otherwise, the New Testament was written in Greek. Some Aramaic expressions were preserved within the Greek original, the most important of which is "Abba," Jesus' word for his Father. In the third century Latin became the language of the Church in Rome and for the most part that of the missionaries who spread the faith from Europe.

These languages are part of our heritage which should be reflected in our liturgy. We need to remember that some familiar words which are part of the Mass are Hebrew, not only "Amen," the universal liturgical word, but "Alleluia" and "Hosanna." On occasion it would be well to substitute the Greek, "Kyrie eleison, Christe eleison, Kyrie eleison" for "Lord have mercy, Christ have mercy, Lord have mercy." A simple sung "Agnus Dei," for the "Lamb of God," can be the Latin part of the Mass. All we

need in addition is Aramaic, especially Jesus' own precious title
for God, "Abba." Do you think we could ever become comfort-
able in praying "Abba in heaven, hallowed be your name"? Some
people are offended by the use of "Father" for God since they
construe it as masculine. They substitute "Good and gracious
God" or "God our Creator," both of which fail to convey Jesus'
revelation that God is the relationship of parent to child. Maybe
"Abba" is the answer.

Ben Jonson wrote of William Shakespeare that he knew a
little Latin and less Greek. Because of our heritage every Catholic ought to know enough to pray a few words, not only in Latin
and Greek, but in Hebrew and Aramaic. And yet, nothing can
substitute for our vernacular, whichever it may be, since our
mother tongue, the language of the heart, is the primary expression of our culture.

Images of Mary

What does a truly Catholic or universal Church look like?
Images of Mary in Catholic art reflect the cultural diversity of
the Church, or at least they should. I must admit there was a
time when I would become upset by Christmas cards which rep-
resented Mary as having blond hair and blue eyes. After all, God
the Creator had formed and fashioned a Semitic maiden of the
tribe of Judah, of the house and family of David, to be the human Mother of his divine Son. I wanted to see Mary on a Christmas card as I envisioned her in my mind: a lovely young girl of
olive smooth complexion, her raven hair parted in the middle
and falling over her shoulders, her dark eyes dancing with the
joy of a new life which had developed within her, the

significance of which even she could not comprehend. At some point I came to realize that my objection to the blond version (dare I say "Hollywood" version) of Mary was a form of fundamentalism. The fact is that Mary was the Jewish mother of the messianic son of David, but the truth goes beyond even that wondrous fact. Mary was the Mother of God. The divine identity of her son moved her to be more than his mother; she became his first and chief disciple and the model of his Church.

Mary is the exemplar for all those who respond to Christ as his faithful disciples, those people who become united with Christ in his mystical body, the Church. Mary, like the Church is Jewish in origin, but like the Church she is universal in essence. The Church does not turn a foreign-looking face to any nation or people. When we remember that the Church is universal, we can see that it is right for people to see Mary as a reflection of themselves. Mary is the Indian-looking Lady of Guadalupe and she is the French-looking Lady of the Miraculous Medal. She is as much Our Lady of Saigon in Vietnam as she is Our Lady of the Angels in Los Angeles. We are not limited to one type of representation of Mary which reflects only a single culture since the Church, of which she is the model, is of various cultures.

Unity and Uniformity

From the very beginning, as we have seen, the Church has struggled to be truly universal. One problem is a failure to make a distinction between unity and uniformity. It is an easy mistake to believe that uniformity is necessary for unity, that Catholics in their worship should all use the same language and follow the same practices so that the Mass would look and sound the same everywhere in the world. The fact is that the Eastern Rite Churches without Latin or any single language, and despite many various ritual traditions, have maintained Catholic unity, whereas Archbishop Lefebvre who insisted on the retention of Latin and the "Tridentine" ritual broke with the Holy See and became schismatic.

The Second Vatican Council in its *Constitution on the Sacred Liturgy* moved to correct the error of equating unity with uniformity by declaring that "Even in the liturgy the Church has no wish to impose a rigid uniformity in matters which do not involve the faith or the good of the whole community. Rather she respects and fosters the spiritual adornments and gifts of the various races and peoples. Provided that the substantial unity of the Roman rite is maintained, the revision of liturgical books should allow for legitimate variations and adaptation to different groups, regions, and peoples, especially in mission lands. Where opportune, the same rule applies to the structuring of rites and the devising of rubrics."[3] In this declaration from the *Constitution* may I please add emphasis to the word "substantial" in the phrase "provided that the *substantial* unity of the Roman rite is maintained…"?

It has remained difficult to achieve adaptations in accord with cultural differences. In fact, when my confrere, Archbishop Annabale Bugnini, C.M., one of the chief architects of Vatican II liturgy, attempted to formulate a concrete plan for cultural adaptations, he was "kicked upstairs" (or downstairs, depending on how you look at it). After having dedicated some forty

---

[3] *Constitution on the Sacred Liturgy*, nos. 37 and 38.

years of his priestly life to the sacred liturgy, he was removed from his position as Secretary of the Congregation for Divine Worship and was made Pro-Nuncio to Iran (!) where he died in 1982.[4]

Conditioning in Culture

In order to be open to the Catholicity of the Church, we must recognize that culture conditions all of us and disposes us to embrace certain values. Some people criticize Padre Junipero Serra, the apostle of California for trying to turn the Indians into Spaniards. Of course he did. How could he have been expected to have done anything else? For him to be Catholic was to be Spanish, just as in a later generation the Irish clergy thought that to be Catholic was to be Irish. Hilaire Belloc, the English Catholic who was born in France, wrote in 1920 that "the Faith is Europe and Europe is the faith."[5] We cannot judge, let alone condemn, people of another era for their cultural conditioning, but after the Vatican Council the limitations of such conditioning can no longer be accepted.

Like everyone, I was conditioned by the religious culture in which I grew up. That was in New Orleans, Louisiana during the 1930's. New Orleans, especially at that time, was a very Catholic city. In fact in our neighborhood there was only one family which was not Catholic. We kids persecuted their little girl. We called her the "Protestant brat." (I drop my head in

---

[4] Archbishop Bugnini wrote a lengthy and fascinating book, *The Reform of the Liturgy, 1948-1975*, which was published by the Liturgical Press.

[5] Hilaire Belloc, *Europe and the Faith*, page 261. Quoted by Mark R. Francis, C.S.V. in *Liturgy in a Multicultural Community*, page 11.

shame as I think about that now.) My father, however, had some business associates who were not Catholic and when the wife of one of them died, I was dragged by my parents to her wake service in the funeral parlor, as we called mortuaries in those days. The room was hushed and in the back someone was playing softly on a small organ. I followed my parents to the front where some object seemed to be the center of attention. It was the casket. My parents stopped and looked at the deceased. As I stood on tip toe to try to see, I heard my mother whisper to my father, "Doesn't she look nice!" Then we went and sat in what resembled a pew. Passive silence reigned. I thought I was in church.

In contrast was my experience when Cardinal Eugenio Pacelli was elected Pope in 1939 (I was just nine years old). No one owned a TV in those days (TV was just being introduced at the New York World's Fair), but we did have Pathe News in the movie theater. I remember vividly seeing the new Pope being carried on the sedia gestatoria into St. Peter's Basilica. The people were going wild, clapping, yelling, and chanting "Viva il Papa!" And I thought, "In church?" I was shocked because during elementary school I used to get in trouble with the nuns at Mass for merely looking across the aisle at the girls. What was scandalous to me because of the Jansenistic atmosphere of my upbringing was perfectly normal, even devout, for the Italians.

One Sunday at St. Julie's Church in Newbury Park, California the newly formed choir remained in the front of the church after Mass, receiving the congratulations of some of the assembly. I was in the rear, greeting the people as they were leaving, when one of them stopped and insisted, "Father, you go up there and tell those people that Catholics do not talk in church!" As pleasantly as possible I explained to her that I could not do so because I was convinced that God the Father was delighted to see his children exchanging pleasantries in his home just as any parents would.

Culture and Reverence

I have found that one of the most controversial aspects of culture revolves around the matter of reverence. These days some people complain that there is no reverence in church by which they mean that the Mass is no longer overlaid by a heavy silence as in the so-called Tridentine Mass. One could answer that reverence is in the heart and the mind of the believer, but the truth is that liturgy by its nature demands that there be external signs of internal sentiments. The liturgy is composed of body as well as soul. External signs of internal reverence are present regardless of one's culture.

The first is that shortly after we have assembled for Mass the priest invites us to acknowledge our sinfulness. A moment of silence follows. This simple act manifests our unworthiness before the infinite holiness of God. It is an act of reverence. During the liturgy of the word we honor Christ present in the holy scriptures. The inspired word is proclaimed from a large book, usually red in color, which by its size and beauty manifests the reverence we owe to Christ present in his word. (Never should the word be proclaimed from a missalette.) To this proclamation of the word we respond by saying "Thanks be to God," and "Praise to you, Lord Jesus Christ." Thanks and praise are sentiments due to Christ in his divinity; they express our reverence.

In the low Mass before the restoration mandated by the

Second Vatican Council, only the priest prayed the "Sanctus," and that silently. Now we all sing or say in response to God's magnificence, "Holy, holy, holy Lord, God of power and might!" The triple "holy," a form of the superlative degree, expresses our profound adoration of the magnificence of God. When we proclaim the mystery of our faith, "Christ has died, Christ is risen, Christ will come again," our hearts should be filled with awe and wonder at the incomprehensible love of Christ for us. We acknowledge that Christ, by his death and resurrection, is the Savior of the world.

Our faith teaches us that Christ is present not only in the inspired word and in the holy Eucharist, but also in his people, who form his mystical body. The sign of peace is a recognition of the presence of Christ in others and an expression of reverence for him. During the sign of peace, we need to remember the words of Jesus, "Whatever you do to even the least of my brothers and sisters, you do to me." In coming to communion we are asked to manifest reverence by bowing to the presence of Christ before we receive the body of the Lord and before we drink from the cup. There is a particularly beautiful sign of reverence when we form our hands into a throne to receive Christ the King.

We may tend to equate reverence with soberness, and to mistake mood for substance. We may yearn for an atmosphere of quiet and reflection. Such we need and must find outside the liturgy. Private devotion is indispensable, but the liturgy is not meant to fulfill that need; liturgy is the celebration of God's family.

Reverence is a form of respect. That word, "respect," comes from the Latin which means "to look again." When we give liturgy a second look, when we respect it for what it truly is, we will recognize that it is meant to take place within the atmosphere of a happy family, the family of God. When we discard the cultural caricature of reverence as solemn and somber rather than as joyful and jubilant, active participation will allow us to experience the profound reverence of Vatican II liturgy.

Indispensable Principles from Vatican II

Not all cultural expressions are acceptable. The *Constitution on the Sacred Liturgy* warns against practices which are "indissolubly bound up with superstition and error."[6] Even practices which, although not superstitious or erroneous, interfere with the proper celebration of liturgy are not to influence our worship. Whatever adaptations for language and culture may be made, the basic principles of Vatican II's *Constitution on the Sacred Liturgy* must be followed. Among the most important of those principles, I suggest the following: "Every liturgical celebration, because it is an action of Christ the priest and of his body, the Church, is a sacred action surpassing all others. No other action of the Church can match its claim to efficacy nor equal the degree of it."[7] There is to be no debate about the importance of the liturgy.

To the liturgy all must come with faith that Christ is present and active in four ways: in his people gathered in his name, in the priest presiding in his person, in his word proclaimed, and in his Eucharist celebrated. Neglecting or minimizing any one of these actions of Christ is unacceptable.

---

[6] *Constitution on the Sacred Liturgy*, no. 37.
[7] *Ibid.*, no. 7.

Because of the importance of the liturgy "Mother Church earnestly desires that all the faithful be led to that full, conscious, and active participation in the liturgical celebration which is demanded by the very nature of the liturgy. Such participation... is their right and duty by reason of their baptism. In the restoration and promotion of the sacred liturgy, this full and active participation by all the people is the aim to be considered before all else, for it is the primary and indispensable source from which the faithful are to derive the true Christian spirit."[8] A passive, "quiet" liturgy is not in accord with the principles of the *Constitution*. The *Constitution* clarifies the nature of active participation: "The people are to be encouraged to take part by means of acclamations, responses, psalmody, antiphons, and songs, as well as by actions, gestures, and bodily attitudes. And at the proper times all should observe a reverent silence."[9] "In liturgical celebrations, all persons should perform their role by doing solely but totally what the nature of things and liturgical norms require of them."

Finally everyone must remember this declaration of the *Constitution*: "Zeal for the promotion and restoration of the liturgy is rightly held to be a sign of the providential disposition of God in our time, as a movement of the Holy Spirit in his Church. It is today a distinguishing mark of the Church's life, indeed of the whole tenor of contemporary religious thought and action."[10]

Paradoxically the Church to be fully Catholic must be freed from a single culture in order to embrace all cultures. Vatican

---

[8] *Ibid.*, no. 17.
[9] *Ibid.*, no. 30.
[10] *Ibid.*, no. 43.

II's *Pastoral Constitution on the Church in the Modern World* declared that "the Church, sent to all peoples of every time and place, is not bound exclusively and indissolubly to any race or nation, nor to any particular way of life or any customary pattern of living, ancient or recent. Faithful to her own tradition and at the same time conscious of her universal mission, she can enter into communion with various cultural modes, to her own enrichment and theirs too."[11]

The Church by embracing all cultures shows forth her beauty and her true character in the multiple images of Mary, the Mother and Model of the Church.

---

[11] *Pastoral Constitution on the Church in the Modern World*, no. 58. It is very enlightening to read all of Chapter II, which is entitled "The Proper Development of Culture."

Chapter 15

The Future

*"For I know well the plans I have in mind for you,
says the Lord, plans for your welfare, not for woe, plans to
give you a future full of hope."* (Jeremiah 29:11)

I HOPE THAT I DO NOT GET INTO trouble for telling this story. I guess I am following the adage that it is easier to ask for forgiveness than for permission. Four nuns were in a car on an L.A. freeway when a cop pulled them over. The cop said, "Sister, you cannot drive so slowly on the freeway. That is very dangerous." The nun objected, "But, officer, all the signs said 25." The cop sighed and said, "Sister, that is not the speed limit. That is the highway number." The nun said, "Oh, that explains why all the sisters were yelling at me before. We just came off highway 101."

In thinking about the future, it is important to read the signs of the times. That expression I associate with Pope John XXIII but it goes back at least to St. Ignatius, the bishop of Antioch, who died around the year 107.[1] Some of what I have to say I believe will happen; others things I think should happen. I trust that what I present is done so modestly.

---

[1] In his letter to St. Polycarp. See the Office of Readings for Friday of the Seventeenth Week of the Year.

Judaizers, Past and Present

The condition of the Church today in many aspects is little different from that of its earliest era. Remember the Judaizers. They resisted the freshness and the radical nature of what Jesus had done and insisted that all Gentile disciples of Jesus had to become Jewish. It took time for the Church to be freed of their error after the decrees of the Council of Jerusalem, but eventually the Judaizers faded away.

Those who resist or, even worse, simply reject the Second Vatican Council are like contemporary Judaizers. Although in most instances they are in good faith, they need to learn that they are not reacting against a sudden, new change in the Church but a slow, deliberate development which was led by the Popes of the past one hundred years. By the grace of God resistance to the Council will evaporate and in a generation nothing more will be heard of it.

Vatican III?

Will there be a Third Vatican Council? Probably, but it may turn out to be the First Council of Kampala in Uganda, or the First of Manila in the Philippines, or the First of Buenos Aires in Argentina. (Other ecumenical councils have been held far from Rome and the Vatican, such as those at Constantinople, Lyons, Ephesus, and Chalcedon.) This is not to imply that the Bishop of Rome will no longer be the head of the Catholic Church but only to suggest that the awareness of our true catholicity may urge a location beyond Italy and Europe. Responding to a profound respect for the various cultures through which authentic Catholicism is expressed, the theme of the Council may well be the truth that unity does not demand uniformity. This will necessitate an investigation into what is essential to the Catholic faith.[2] This investigation will allow and foster cultural expressions in the liturgy as the norm. It will also lead to a cognate topic, ecumenism. The Council through its understanding of what is essential to authentic Catholicism, and especially what is not, will make strides toward ending the scandal of division within Christendom. It will establish means for unity first with the Orthodox, secondly with the Anglicans, and then with the mainstream Protestants.

If it seems bold to make these assertions, I can only appeal to the fact that the seeds of the next Council are found in the *Decree on Ecumenism*, as well as in the *Constitution on the Sacred Liturgy*, especially in the section on "Norms for Adapting the Liturgy to the Genius and Traditions of Peoples" (paragraphs 37 through 40).

Meanwhile National Conferences of Bishops need to be granted more responsibility and authority for the liturgy in their own regions. It was quite inappropriate that the United States Bishops had to struggle with Vatican authorities to return to the practice of communion in the hand, to allow girls and women to be ministers at the altar, and to make such minor changes as the use of the single word "all" during the consecration of the wine ("it will be shed for you and for all," omitting the word "men"). The Conference of American Bishops is quite competent to decide how much use to make of inclusive language,

---

[2] Pope Paul VI made a modest beginning in this matter in his encyclical on evangelization, *Evangelii Nuntiandi*, in Chapter III on "The Content of Evangelization."

whether in liturgical prayers or in scriptural translations, and to form policies regarding their own language and customs. All concerned must remember that the Council declared that "Even in the liturgy the Church has no wish to impose a rigid uniformity in matters which do not involve the faith or the good of the whole community." To Conferences of Bishops applies the teaching of the Council that "all the faithful, clerical and lay, possess a lawful freedom of inquiry and thought, and the freedom to express their minds humbly and courageously about those matters in which they enjoy competence."[3]

For the sake of the sacramental life of the Church it will, or should, be left to National Conferences of Bishops to determine suitable candidates for the priesthood, especially in accord with the practice of ordaining married men in the early Church. I must emphasize that there is a difference between allowing priests to get married, for which there is no tradition in the Church, and choosing to ordain married men, for which there is a precedent not only in the Eastern Churches outside the United States to this day but in the ancient Church in general. Objections to a married clergy dissolve when we recognize that there is nothing inherently objectionable to ordaining mature married men, whose children are grown and whose marriages are stable, and who are the respected leaders in their parishes. In my experience there are men like that in almost every parish. A sober observance of the signs of the times leads one to conclude that the ordination of women, even as deacons, does not seem to be part of the foreseeable future but the ministry of women flowing from their baptism should not be merely tol-

---

[3] *Pastoral Constitution on the Church in the Modern World*, no. 62.

erated but positively fostered. As it is, in the vast majority of parishes in the United States about eighty percent of ministry is performed by women. Their generous spirit deserves to be appreciated and supported.

Implementing Vatican II

Until the Church meets again in Council, or maybe I should say before it can, we must proceed with implementing the Second Vatican Council, the regressive and the recalcitrant to the contrary notwithstanding. The Vatican Council was, to repeat Rahner's insight, "the Church's first official self-actualization as a world Church." We must not be the Judaizers of our day. It is not right to go backwards. A declaration found in the *Constitution on the Sacred Liturgy* (no. 43) could be applied, *mutatis mutandis*, to all the work of the Council: "Zeal for the promotion and restoration of the sacred liturgy is rightly held to be a sign of the providential movement of the Holy Spirit in the Church. Today it is a distinguishing mark of the Church's life, indeed of the whole tenor of contemporary religious thought and action."

The movement of the Holy Spirit in preparing for the Council was slow and deliberate. It only seemed abrupt because of a failure to keep Catholics abreast of the developments in the Church. While we lament that failure and even repent of it, we must not allow its results to deter us. Now is the time for all Catholics, not to continue to be dismayed by changes or to resist them, and certainly not to attempt to return to the era before the Council, but to proceed faithfully in accord with the guidance of the Holy Spirit in the Church.

*　*　*

This concludes Volume Three. Volume One is on Foundations of Vatican II Liturgy and Volume Two is on the Celebration of the Eucharist. If you have not read these two books, I hope you will do so now. If you wish to have a quartet, you may acquire from Alba House my book on the Liturgy of the Hours, *Together in Prayer.*